# FINANCIAL SECURITY
# IN TROUBLED TIMES

# FINANCIAL SECURITY IN TROUBLED TIMES

## What You Need to Do Now

### RIC EDELMAN

HarperBusiness
*An Imprint of* HarperCollins*Publishers*

This book contains historical performance data. Presentation of performance data does not imply that similar results will be achieved in the future. Rather, past performance is no indication of future results and any assertion to the contrary is a federal offense. Any such data is provided merely for illustrative and discussion purposes; rather than focusing on the time periods used or the results derived, the reader should focus on the underlying principles.

None of the material presented here is intended to serve as the basis for any financial decision, nor does any of the information contained within constitute an offer to buy or sell any security. Such an offer is made only by prospectus, which you should read carefully before investing or sending money.

The material presented in this book is accurate to the best of my knowledge. However, performance data changes over time, and laws frequently change as well, and my advice could change accordingly. Therefore, the reader is encouraged to verify the status of such information before acting.

The author and the publisher expressly disclaim liability for any losses that may be sustained by the use of the material in this book.

FINANCIAL SECURITY IN TROUBLED TIMES. Copyright © 2001 by Ric Edelman. All rights reserved. Printed in the United States of America. No part of this book may be used or reproduced in any manner whatsoever without written permission except in the case of brief quotations embodied in critical articles and reviews. For information, address HarperCollinsPublishers, Inc., 10 East 53rd Street, New York, NY 10022.

FIRST EDITION

Production by Stratford Publishing Services, Brattleboro, Vermont

Library of Congress Cataloging-in-Publication data have been applied for.

ISBN 0-06-009403-6

*This book is dedicated to the people who died
in the September 11 attacks, and to their families.*

*May God bless them all.*

# CONTENTS

# ACKNOWLEDGMENTS

ALTHOUGH WRITING is supposed to be a solitary endeavor, nothing I do ever occurs in isolation. I am grateful to John Davis, Jerry Mason, Carol Roberts, and Robin Thompson for their research assitance; to Mike Attiliis, Jack Bubon, Mary Davis, Dutch Fox, Joe Gilmore, and Ed Moore for their fast reading of the manuscript Monday morning, mere hours before the Harper-Collins production deadline; and to Will Casserly, Jerry Mason, and Evy Sheehan for helping me proof the final pages.

Thanks also to David Conti, my editor, for helping me keep the manuscript on track—and for keeping his comments and suggestions short. He offered lots of great advice, and I could tell he wanted to say more than he did.

A special thank you to Cathy Hemming, publisher of Harper-Collins, for her willingness to devote all her corporate resources to the publication of this book, so that we could provide this information to Americans across the country as quickly as possible. I am impressed with her leadership and humbled by her commitment to community service.

As always, I am most grateful to my wife, Jean, who unfailingly and lovingly supports me every time I go and do something crazy, like write a book in two days.

# INTRODUCTION

Not long ago, America was going about its business. The fall TV shows were being launched, as was the new football season. People were fretting over their tech stocks and wondering if the stock market was poised for a recovery. Kids were back in the classroom, fresh from the summer off. Life was normal.

Then came September 11 and the horrible attack on this country by cowards.

In the aftermath of that terrible day, people have begun to wonder about the safety and security of their families and homes, their jobs, and their investments. The attacks disrupted every facet of our society. We wonder when life will return to normal, and if it ever will.

And yet, through all this, Americans have come together like never before, with a patriotic unity that has surprised our enemies and instilled fear in them. The entire civilized world shares our sorrow, and our resolve.

As our nation moves toward the eradication of this evil throughout the world, we Americans also need to act individually to protect and secure our own lives, those of our families, and those within our communities. The rules have changed, and we must reevaluate what we've been doing and how we've been doing it.

Change is unsettling, but in these times unavoidable. And feeling unsettled is the least of the emotions we've all felt in the weeks since September 11.

I mention that because this is a book about emotions. That might seem strange to say; after all, you're reading this book for its financial advice, and it is written by a financial advisor. But the truth is that personal finance is entirely about emotion, because how you feel determines how you behave. And because the horrific events of September 11 raised such powerful emotions in all of us, they are where we must begin.

We must understand what we're feeling and realize that our emotions could hurt us—or help us.

So, yes, this book is about emotions. But it's also a focused conversation on money. I'll show you what to do now to maximize your family's financial security in these troubled times and to help you prepare for the prosperity that is coming. Those who position themselves today for that prosperity will be the ones to enjoy it, and you can be among them.

This is not the time for worry. It's the time for positive action. This book will show you what to do *right now*, so read it quickly and act immediately—for the benefit of yourself, your family, your community, and our nation.

Some readers may be wondering how I could have written this book so quickly.

How could I *not* have? My life is devoted to providing people with financial advice, and today people need that kind of advice more than ever. Our world has been turned upside down, and we're all wondering what the new rules are, and which strategies to adopt to provide our families with security, safety, and prosperity.

It's clear that people can't wait months or years for this information. They need it *now*. So, on September 24, less than two weeks after the attack on America, HarperCollins agreed to publish a book that gives people the advice they now need. Recognizing the urgency, HarperCollins agreed to speed the book into stores as quickly as possible, and I decided to give all my profits from the sale of this book to relief efforts and other charities.

Now, all I had to do was write it. I started that Friday night, and by 1:00 A.M. Monday, it was done.

The book tells you how to handle your cash, your mortgage, your job, and your investments. It explains how to protect yourself, your family, your home, your car, and your company. It reminds us of our need to help each other and shows you how to do that. Writing quickly (and late into the night), I may not have expressed everything perfectly or covered every topic as completely as a long, leisurely schedule would have allowed. Nonetheless, the information you'll find in these pages will help you protect yourself and your family *right now*. I hope you'll read it as quickly as I wrote it, because just as America as a nation needs to act immediately and decisively, so do you. This book is intended to return you to the basics, to help you put into today's context all the aspects of your personal finances that you've ignored, avoided, or failed to know about. That's because now more than ever, you must tend to these fundamentals, because the best way to succeed in troubled times is to make sure you have all the basics covered, and this book will help you do that.

Like all Americans, I've wanted to do something to help. I can't help the firefighters search through the rubble. But I can offer financial advice, and I can raise money to help the cause, so that's what I've done.

## CHAPTER 1

# You're Not Alone

THE SEPTEMBER 11 ATTACK ON AMERICA remains incomprehensible.

Disbelief and shock have given way to horror, sadness, fear, and anger. In the days after the hijackings and attacks on the World Trade Center and Pentagon that were made by hate-filled cowards—I refuse to call them terrorists—many Americans began to feel inept. We didn't know how to help, where to send money, who to assist. The realization that we face an anonymous enemy intensified our frustration at our apparent inability to do something constructive.

That's a lot of emotions to pack into a short period. Tell me, did you feel any of these emotions:

- disbelief,
- shock,
- horror,
- sadness,
- fear,
- anger?

I've been presenting lots of seminars since the attack, teaching people what to do now about their finances, and I've asked every audience about their emotions. Just about all the people I've met have said they've been feeling *all of the above*. Furthermore, many people have told me that they didn't realize others were feeling the same way. I share all this with you because it may comfort you to know you're not alone in this tragedy.

Let's take this a step further. Since the events of September 11,

- Have your sleep habits changed? Many people have had insomnia, while others have talked of exhaustion that has caused them to sleep more than usual. Many also report unusually active dreaming, including nightmares.
- Has your appetite changed? Many people now have little desire for food, while others are bingeing—they can't get enough chocolate!

It's also quite possible that you are feeling nothing at all. Many have told me that since the attack, they have felt *numb*. This, too, is remarkably common and quite understandable: Trying to process all the information can lead to sensory overload, and for many, it has been so overwhelming that we don't know what to feel. Many people have felt simply dazed.

One of my staff entered a grocery store a few days after the attack. The store wasn't crowded, and she noticed that no one offered eye contact. The mood was sullen. No one was talking. When she got to the checkout counter, the clerk told her to be sure to take her packages home. To her confused expression, he responded, "We've noticed that people are coming through the line, paying for their purchases, putting their bags into their cart and taking their cart out to the curb. Then they get into their cars and drive away—leaving their bags here."

This absentmindedness is all too easy to understand.

Perhaps the most common feeling is profound loss. Many people who didn't know one of the victims personally know someone who did. We all have stories to tell. One of my firm's clients perished in the attack; he was in the plane that hit the Pentagon. My wife's cousin was in the World Trade Center during the attack; we are thankful that she was able to escape. And I was in the WTC just a few days before September 11. Because so many of us can relate to stories like this, and because we will be hearing these stories forever, it is natural for us to believe that our lives have changed forever.

Psychologists, therapists, and grief counselors will tell you that all of the emotions we are experiencing are natural stages of grief. What's most important is that you understand that it's okay to have these feelings and that you're not alone. Indeed, we are all feeling this same way.

I mention all this—this is a book on personal finance, remember?—because there is one particular emotion we haven't considered that requires your immediate consideration.

That emotion?

Guilt.

I'm not saying that you should feel guilty about the attack or that you have any responsibility for or involvement in the tragic loss of life. No, when I refer to guilt, I mean the following. Since September 11, have you:

- Gone shopping?
- Been to the movies?
- Eaten in a restaurant?
- Traveled to another city?
- Attended routine events, such as PTA or civic meetings?

As we all know, airports, shopping malls, schools, museums, and sports complexes—every public building—closed immediately after the attack. Even after the stores reopened, they remained empty of customers. One common reason for this: Many people feel guilty shopping. After all, how can I do something as mundane and *selfish* as buying a sweater or seeing a movie, while others around me are struggling to cope with the horrible loss of life?

It is easy to understand why people would feel self-conscious, if not downright guilty, about carrying on their normal lives in this most abnormal of times. But it's essential that you do exactly that.

Your community needs you to do so. We all know that millions of American workers live paycheck to paycheck. In the aftermath of the attacks, many of those paychecks have stopped. I'm not talking only about the financial problems now facing the airline, travel and hospitality, and insurance industries.

I'm talking about commissioned-based workers. Most people think of car salesmen when they hear that phrase, but it goes much deeper than that: A huge portion of American workers earn commission-based compensation.

Cab drivers, for instance. Cabbies in New York went more than a week without a fare—and no fares means no paycheck.

Restaurant workers are struggling: If you don't go into a restaurant, the waiter makes no money. Ditto for the busboy, chefs, and the young lady who takes reservations and greets you at the door.

Hotel staffs are in economic jeopardy. Thousands of meetings, conferences, and conventions were canceled after the attack. Now, in hotels across the country, housekeeping staffs have no rooms that need cleaning, caterers have no meals that need serving, bellboys have no luggage that needs toting, and doormen have no cabs that need hailing.

At airports and in downtowns all over America, workers depend on daily business for financial survival. With few airplane passengers, airport skycaps are going broke. With tourists scarce, street vendors are struggling. And if you haven't visited your local drycleaner or convenience store, or grabbed your usual cappuccino en route to work, *you* are causing the backbone of the American economy to break.

We've seen the results: Airlines have laid off tens of thousands of workers, hotels have cut staff by 50% or more in many cities, and restaurants are nearly empty. If we want to show the cowards that they have failed, we must return to our normal routines. And that means, among other things, that *we must go shopping*.

So, my first—and most important—piece of financial advice to you is this:

**H**ug your family, wave a flag, light a candle, go to church, say a prayer, give blood, make a donation, *and spend some of your money*.

I realize that you don't feel like spending money—but I want you to do so anyway. I also realize that you resist spending money for practical reasons, and we'll examine those issues later in this book. But it's important to keep in mind that you've gone back to work or school even though you didn't feel like it, and that was the much-needed first step toward returning to normalcy. The next step is to go back into the stores and restaurants. Do so today.

## CHAPTER 2

# You Need Cash Reserves

I ADMIT I WAS SKEPTICAL when Richard Grasso, chair of the New York Stock Exchange, announced that the stock market would reopen the Monday after the attack. I was skeptical simply because of my familiarity with Wall Street. With the downtown area closed to cars, buses, and subways, it seemed to me a daunting task to get tens of thousands of people into place by 9:30 that Monday morning. Everyone knew that many of the telecommunications systems had been knocked out, but I was more concerned about how the NYSE was going to feed all those workers—after all, none of the surrounding businesses would be open, even if the NYSE was in full operation!

And yet, despite these incredible logistical challenges, New York pulled it off, and that first day of trading went smoothly. In fact, the NYSE had a record day: More than 2.4 billion shares were traded. This was a wonderful, heartening testament to the determination of New Yorkers.

Although the financial markets are now back in full operation, we cannot ignore the fact that for four days, the markets were closed. During this time, every investment account in the nation was frozen. Whether you have a mutual fund account, a retirement account at work, an IRA, or a brokerage account, it was frozen.

This is an important point, because financial advisors like me often tout the benefits of mutual funds. We say they are diversified, professionally managed, safe compared to many other types of investments, and *liquid*.

I'm sure you've heard that word before. *Liquid*. In Wall Street parlance, *liquidity* refers to your ability to access your money. With highly liquid investments, you can access your money any time you want. Bank accounts are in this category—just write a check!

Mutual funds are also considered liquid, though less so than bank accounts. That's because it takes a few days for a mutual fund company to send you a check once you request it. And, unlike bank accounts, mutual fund values fluctuate daily. Despite these issues, though, mutual funds are considered liquid investments, as are stocks and bonds.

In contrast, real estate is considered an illiquid investment. Whereas selling a mutual fund requires only a phone call or email, real estate can take weeks, even months, to sell.

On September 11, *liquidity* was redefined.

## IS YOUR INVESTMENT INCOME SAFE?

We all were reminded on that day that our mutual fund and brokerage accounts can be rendered as illiquid as real estate. Bank accounts can be frozen, too, although this didn't happen in the wake of the recent attack. (It last happened on March 6, 1933, when Franklin Roosevelt declared a three-day "bank holiday" at the height of the Depression.)

For most American investors, the market's four-day closing was inconsequential—perhaps even beneficial. After all, by not being able to trade, investors were unable to sell during the worst of their emotional insecurity. The delay in trading for nearly a week gave investors a chance to calm down. Besides, most investors didn't really need to trade during that week. So what if you had to wait a few days to buy Acme Widgets or sell Ajax Hoozits? For most investors, the market's closing was more a conversation topic than an impact.

But there are some investors for whom the shutdown was a problem. For these investors, the failure to reopen the markets quickly could have become a personal financial crisis.

Who are these people? They are retirees and others who receive monthly income from their investments. Although most investors are socking away money for their future, for retirees the future is now. They live off the income their investments generate. They receive dividend income, interest income, and income from capital gains.

When retirees establish mutual fund accounts, they often instruct the fund to send them a monthly check. Called a "systematic withdrawal," these checks go out to account holders on the 1st, the 15th, or the 30th of every month.

The checks due September 15 didn't arrive.

They couldn't. Not only was September 15 a Saturday, meaning transactions would be posted on Monday, but the markets were closed from the 11th through the 16th. Realizing the potential interruption that some of our clients might be facing, we quickly contacted the mutual fund companies that held our clients' assets, verified the status of their distributions, and contacted our clients with the news.

The news was good: Because the markets were scheduled to reopen on the 17th, the checks would be delayed by only a few days. All our clients who were due to receive checks on the 15th got them by the 19th. No one missed a mortgage payment.

This time.

This is why you need cash reserves. You need to have money readily available to you in case a check you're expecting fails to arrive. This time, the checks were delayed because the markets were closed for logistic reasons, not because of nationwide financial panic, government instability, or economic uncertainty. The result was the same, however: Mutual fund companies were unable to execute liquidation requests, even routine ones like monthly redemptions for retirees.

Next time, the delay might be caused by something as mundane as a disruption in mail service or as dramatic as the failure of a financial institution.

Ironically, I had warned of this risk on my weekly radio show just three weeks before the cowardly attack on America. As I explained then, most people do not understand that mutual funds have the legal right to withhold liquidation requests. It takes extraordinarily rare circumstances, but it does happen. For example, in 2000, one mutual fund managed to lose 70% in a single day. Amazingly, this fund was not invested in tech stocks—in fact, it wasn't even a stock fund! It was a fund that invested in *municipal bonds*.

Most people consider muni bonds to be among the safest investments. After all, most are government guaranteed. But this particular fund had bought muni bonds that were not guaranteed. Instead, the bonds had been issued by state agencies that weren't even rated by muni bond rating services. The fund's management began to realize that nobody really knew what these bonds were worth in the marketplace, and the manager decided to reprice the bonds. He cut their value by 70%, literally overnight.

As you can imagine, that move angered the shareholders, who responded by filing more than 20 class action lawsuits. Federal regulators are still investigating.

But get this: The regulators have frozen the fund's assets while it's under investigation. For more than a year now monthly dividends have stopped and no one has been allowed to redeem his or her money.

I mention this to remind you that it is possible—however unlikely—that your mutual fund might not promptly execute a redemption request.

Makes you question the meaning of "liquid investment," doesn't it?

## IS YOUR PAYCHECK SAFE?

Even if you're not receiving income from your investments, you still need cash reserves. Why? Because your next paycheck might never arrive. Hundreds of thousands of New Yorkers found themselves unable to go to work in the days after September 11. Thousands of businesses were closed. With no revenue, these businesses found it difficult, if not impossible, to pay their employees. If you were one of them, you suddenly had a problem.

## HOW MUCH CASH TO KEEP IN RESERVE

So whether your income comes from pensions, investments, or a paycheck, it's important that you maintain cash reserves. Ordinarily, financial planners like me encourage consumers to maintain cash reserves in case your car breaks down or the roof leaks. After all, as I said in *The Truth About Money*, you need cash reserves because every single day in America, 15,000 washing machines break down (according to Sears, which sells more washing machines than anyone).

The calamity of September 11 has caused us to renew our emphasis on this mundane topic. Until September 11, we generally advised that the amount you should keep in reserves depended on two factors: your monthly expenses and the stability of your income. Now we discount the stability of your income, because if there's anything that the tragedy showed us, it's that *no one's income is safe.*

Therefore, I want you to determine how much money you spend each month. One way to do that is to simply look at your checkbook. The problem with this method, though, is that your checkbook might not fully reflect credit card charges or expenses that occur sporadically (such as annual tax or insurance bills).

So let's track your monthly expenses more effectively. To do this, review your checkbook and credit card statements for the past six months, ignoring any one-time or other nonrecurring expenses. This will give you a much more accurate picture of your actual expenses. For more on tracking expenses, see Chapter 51 of *The Truth About Money*.

**K**eep in cash reserves a minimum of three months' worth of spending, and preferably six months'. If your income is very uncertain, you might want to increase your reserves to a full year's worth of expenses.

Please note that if you plan to incur a large expense within the next two years, such as home improvements, the purchase of a car, wedding or college costs, or other big-ticket expenses, you should set aside money for these expenses *in addition to your cash reserves*. Your goal is to maintain reserves at a fully funded level at all times. And, if some crisis does force you to dip into your reserves, your first task is to build them back up again.

## WHERE TO KEEP YOUR
## CASH RESERVES—AND WHERE NOT TO

Once you determine how much you ought to place into cash reserves, make sure you stash that cash—and leave it alone. Never touch your reserves unless you incur a crisis, just as you'd never touch your umbrella unless it started raining.

There are six places you can stash your cash:

- your mattress,
- checking accounts,
- savings accounts,
- money market funds,
- short-term bank CDs,
- U.S. Treasury bills.

Each location has its pitfalls. Money under your mattress is the ultimate in liquidity—and the easiest to lose. Fire and theft—or even a paper-eating dog like my weimaraner, Liza—can render the cash in your house unavailable when you need it. Because money market funds are operated by mutual fund companies, these accounts can be frozen unexpectedly, as they were right after September 11. Bank accounts, too, can be closed, like they were in 1933. So, there's no perfect answer, but it's the best we've got to offer.

For a variety of reasons, including liquidation costs and taxes, the following are not suitable places to put your cash reserves:

- U.S. Treasury notes,
- U.S. Treasury bonds,
- EE savings bonds,
- commercial paper,
- insurance policies,
- fixed annuities.

If you don't have the cash reserves you now realize you need, it would be prudent to raise the cash—even if it means selling or repositioning your investments to do so. Selling mutual funds, stocks, bonds, and real estate might not be the smartest investment strategy—especially if selling would force you to incur transaction costs and taxes or if prices are currently depressed—but I'm not talking about investment strategies here. I'm talking about your *survival*.

If you don't have investments you can sell, consider what you do have. Baseball cards? Used video game collection? Get creative—and serious about tending to your family's financial future.

## YOUR CASH MANAGEMENT SYSTEM

Cash reserves are part of a complete cash management system, which includes checking accounts, savings accounts, and credit cards.

Please do not rely on credit cards or lines of credit as a replacement for cash reserves. They're good to have, but they should complement, not replace, your cash reserves. After all, the first thing a financial institution will do in a crisis is cancel outstanding lines of credit. Remember, in a crisis, cash is king.

Does your cash management system work as it should? To find out, answer these questions:

1. Does all your money earn interest all the time?
2. Do you pay off every credit card balance in full each month?
3. Do you know the approximate balance in your checking account right now?
4. Do you routinely avoid bank and credit card fees?

If you answered yes to all of these questions, your cash management system is working well. If you answered no to any question, you need to make some improvements. As we explore the elements of a cash management system, look for ways that you can improve yours.

### Checking Accounts

Your checking account is the heart of your cash management system, because most of your money flows through it.

## *Types of Checking Accounts*

As simple as they are, checking accounts (also known as demand deposits) come in several varieties:

STUDENT ACCOUNT: Only small deposits are needed to open this account. The monthly charge is small, but banks usually limit the number of checks that you can write each month without a fee.

REGULAR ACCOUNT: There is a monthly charge assessed on this account, sometimes based on the number of checks written during the month.

INTEREST-EARNING ACCOUNT (often referred to as a Negotiable Order of Deposit or NOW account): The money in this account earns interest if the balance exceeds a minimum requirement, but you usually pay a service charge if the balance falls below that minimum.

SPECIAL ACCOUNT: This type of account may not charge a monthly fee, but you pay for each deposit you make and check you write. No minimum balance is required.

## *How Banks Compute the Minimum Balance*

Most financial institutions use one of these two methods to compute the minimum balance in a checking account:

- **Minimum daily balance.** If your balance falls below the bank's minimum requirement once during the month, service charges of $5 to $20 are assessed. Most banks use this method.
- **Average daily balance.** The bank totals the closing balance at the end of each day and divides that total by 30. No service charge is assessed if the monthly average is above the required minimum.

### Endorse Checks Carefully

If you sign your name (called "endorsing") on the back of a check, anyone who finds it can cash it. Therefore, always endorse checks in one of these two ways:

- **Special endorsement.** On the back of the check, write "Pay only [name of payee]" and then sign your name below that statement. This way, only the person you've named can deposit or cash the check.
- **Restrictive endorsement.** On the back of the check, write "For deposit only [your account number]" and then sign your name below that statement. This way, the check can be deposited only into your account.

### Bouncing Checks

A check bounces when there is not enough money in the account to clear it. This is technically called an "overdraft." Bounced checks are stamped "insufficient funds" and returned to the merchant, and your checking account is charged $15 to $40.

Watch out for the domino effect from a bounced check. When you bounce a check, bank fees are immediately withdrawn, reducing the amount of money available in your account and causing more checks to bounce. Banks are also sometimes accused of letting one large check clear so they can then charge bounced-check fees to many smaller checks. Watch your balances carefully to avoid these problems.

Merchants who get back "rubber" checks can redeposit them, and most do. If the check bounces again, your account is charged again. If the check bounces three times, the bank punches holes in the check, making it impossible to redeposit.

Bank officers, if asked, will usually waive the bounced-check fee the *first* time you bounce a check, but if you repeat the error, the bank will not be so accommodating. They may even close your account, and other banks may refuse to let you open a new one.

## Preventing Checks from Bouncing

You can prevent checks from bouncing by asking your bank to activate an automatic funds transfer program. Then the bank will automatically borrow from your credit card to cover a bounced check. Before you agree to this program, consider the following:

1. The bank may charge you a monthly fee for the service, even if you never use it.
2. Funds are deposited from the credit card to your checking account in increments of $100 or $500. Make sure your credit card can handle the expense.
3. You will incur your card's cash advance fee.
4. You start to pay interest on the cash advance from the date your bank transfers funds from the card.
5. Overdraft protection could cause you to accumulate credit card debt.

## Test Your Checking Account

Can your checking account pass this test?

| Your checking account: | Yes | No |
| --- | --- | --- |
| Pays interest on the money in your account. | ___ | ___ |
| Does not charge fees for transactions. | ___ | ___ |
| Does not charge a monthly service charge. | ___ | ___ |
| Offers a free ATM card. | ___ | ___ |
| Does not charge for using your ATM card at its machines. | ___ | ___ |
| Does not charge for printing checks. | ___ | ___ |
| Offers cashier's checks for free. | ___ | ___ |
| Charges only a small fee when you bounce a check. | ___ | ___ |
| Levies no fee for requesting a stop-payment order. | ___ | ___ |
| Levies no fee for transferring funds from one account to another. | ___ | ___ |

Each answer should be yes.

How well did your checking account measure up? If you're not happy with your account, ask your bank to lower or eliminate charges or increase services. If the bank knows you're preparing to leave, it might offer inducements to keep your business.

### Paying for Checks

You are not required to buy checks from your bank. Obtaining them elsewhere might save you a lot of money. Forget about designer checks—are you really trying to impress the phone company?—and put that money to better use.

### Do You Have a Debit Card?

Debit cards look like credit cards, but when you use them, your checking account is immediately debited.

Usually when you use a debit card, you must key in a personal identification number (PIN). When you select a PIN for your debit card, avoid using your birth date, address, or part of your Social Security number. *Never write your PIN anywhere.*

If you report a lost or stolen debit card within 48 hours, your liability is capped at $50. From the 3rd to the 60th day, your liability is $500. If after 60 days you still have not reported the card missing, your liability is unlimited—meaning you could lose all the money you have in the bank, including not just the money in your checking account, but all the money in your savings account, too, if the savings account provides overdraft protection for your checking account. And if you have a home equity loan that you can access through your checking account, a thief who steals your ATM card could withdraw the entire balance of your home equity loan.

**B**e very careful with debit and ATM cards. Secure them carefully.

### *Tips on Properly Using your Checking Account*

1. Never deposit cash in an ATM machine! These dollars can disappear, and you have no proof that you made the deposit. The receipt provided by the ATM is worthless, because you can input any figure into the machine.
2. Endorse checks using black or blue ink.
3. As soon as you receive a check, endorse it using a special or restrictive endorsement.
4. Remember that *tomorrow* is the soonest that checks deposited today are credited to your account. Many people incorrectly assume that because they just made a deposit at an ATM machine, they can now spend the funds. Not possible! ATM *withdrawals* are immediately subtracted from your account, but *deposits* are not credited for up to four days.

## Savings Accounts

Savings accounts, also known as time deposits, are ideal for storing money you will need as soon as tomorrow or perhaps not for three years. Interest earned on such accounts is terribly low, and varies little from institution to institution, so choose your account for its convenience and other services.

A new "Truth in Savings" law requires your financial institution to tell you about:

- fees that could be assessed against savings accounts,
- the interest rate the account pays,
- the Annual Percentage Yield. This reveals how much $100 would earn in interest if the $100 was left with the bank for a year. The APY makes it easy to compare rates among financial institutions.

## Three Risks of Having Money in Savings Accounts

Savings accounts are very safe places for your cash reserves, but there *are* a few risks:

INFLATION: A dollar buys more today than it will tomorrow, because the cost of goods and services tends to rise over time. If the interest rate your account pays is less than the rate of inflation, you're actually losing money—in terms of buying power—by keeping money in the account.

TAXATION: Uncle Sam taxes the interest you earn in a savings account.

SAFETY: Accounts are insured only up to $100,000, and even this protection is meaningless if there is a "run" on the banks, like there was in the Great Depression.

## Consider Credit Unions

Often the best deals for both checking and savings accounts are offered by credit unions. As nonprofit organizations, they typically pay higher rates on checking and savings accounts and charge lower rates on loans.

If you do not belong to a credit union and want to see if you're eligible to join one in your area, call the Credit Union National Association at 1-800-358-5710.

## Using Your Savings Account to Boost Your Wealth

1. On the day before payday, deposit any money you have left in your checking account (in excess of the minimum required balance) to a savings account.
2. Each month, have funds automatically transferred from your checking account to your savings account to fund a short-term goal or nonmonthly expenses such as annual insurance premiums or vacations.

3. When you finish paying off your car loan, continue depositing the loan payment into a savings account to accumulate money for your next car.
4. When you get a raise, save or invest the increased income, instead of spending it.
5. Get a part-time job and set aside the take-home pay to fund a specific goal.

## How Safe Are Safes?

Most financial institutions offer safe deposit boxes. They can be great places to keep items that are difficult or impossible to replace, such as:

- jewelry,
- real estate deeds,
- photos and negatives,
- videos of your personal possessions,
- valuable items from collections,
- legal documents,
- birth, marriage, and death certificates,
- stock and bond certificates.

Certain original documents should *not* be placed in a safe deposit box. These include:

- passports,
- wills,
- trust documents,
- Living Wills or Medical Directives,
- powers of Attorney,
- insurance policies.

You never want to keep these items in a safe deposit box, because you might need access to them while the institution is closed.

Furthermore, your box might be sealed by the bank upon your death, preventing your family from accessing wills and insurance policies (see next section). Therefore, you should maintain these types of papers in a fire- and burglar-proof home safe (see Home Safe Home).

Although the originals of the documents listed above should not be placed into a safe deposit box, you can—and should—place copies of these documents there.

ACCESS TO YOUR SAFE DEPOSIT BOX: State law determines who has access to your safe deposit box after your death. A person's safe deposit box is often sealed after his or her death because the state wants to prevent the box's contents from disappearing before tax authorities arrive.

Therefore, when you apply for a box, ask who is permitted to access it after your death, and under what circumstances. Often, the only person who has access to the box is the person who jointly rents it with you. People whom you have given Power of Attorney (see Chapter 6) are often prohibited from opening your box, even if they have the key.

Others can gain access to your box (or prevent you from removing items from it) if you:

1. Owe a judgment from a court case.
2. Owe the IRS back taxes.
3. Are thought to be hiding stolen items.

HOW SAFE IS A SAFE DEPOSIT BOX? The contents are protected from fire, flood, earthquakes, and other natural disasters, but they are not *completely* protected from these calamities—nothing is. And institutions do not guarantee to reimburse you for the contents if they are lost though a natural (or other) disaster.

Your bank is also not likely to carry any insurance protecting the contents of your safe deposit box. You may get such coverage from your homeowner's policy (see Chapter 5), but talk with your insurance agent to be certain.

## Home Safe Home

Maybe a bank safe deposit box is not the perfect solution for protecting all the valuables that are difficult or impossible to replace. Consider a home safe. Those who sell safes tout these advantages:

- A safe will secure and protect your valuables and priceless items from fire and burglary.
- A safe gives you a definite location to place all your precious belongings. You'll never misplace an item again or waste time looking for your special hiding place.
- By choosing a safe over a bank deposit box, you enjoy the convenience of having your most precious possessions nearby, while avoiding the expense of renting a box.

These benefits are accurate—*if* you know a little bit more about safes. Most burglar safes offer a degree of fire protection, but fire safes can be opened in less than five minutes with ordinary tools. Therefore, you want a safe that will protect your possessions from fire *and* burglars.

Ignore general claims that a safe is burglary or fire resistant, because such terms are meaningless. Only ratings by an independent organization such as Underwriter's Laboratories (UL) can be relied on.

WHAT THE RATINGS TELL YOU ABOUT A HOME SAFE: The safe's internal heat buildup is rated as:

- **UL 350–1:** The heat inside the safe will not exceed 350 degrees during the first hour.
- **UL 350–2:** The safe provides two hours of such protection.

UL 350 should be adequate protection for most papers, but if you plan to store photos, videotape, or magnetic tape, you should obtain a safe rated UL 150.

The safe's ability to withstand tampering is measured as:

- **TL 15:** Using common tools, a thief cannot open the safe for 15 minutes.
- **TL 30:** A burglar cannot open the safe for 30 minutes.

A rating that includes "TR" means the safe also resists cutting torches. Safes of lower quality are labeled "B" or "C" and are less expensive, but they provide less protection.

TYPES OF HOME SAFES: Hollywood has popularized wall safes hidden behind pictures, but these are easy to open. Besides, the burglar can just yank the safe out of the wall and take it home.

Heavy safes that are bolted to the floor are often burglar and fire proof, but safes installed *in* the floor give the best protection (especially if installed in concrete).

---

**Y**ou have precious and valuable items that you cannot replace. Buy a home safe for them and keep an inventory of these items elsewhere.

---

## CHAPTER 3

# You Need a Mortgage More Than Ever

FOR MORE THAN A DECADE, I have urged Americans to carry a big, long mortgage—a 30-year loan that's as big as you can get. I have been associated with this financial strategy more than any other financial advisor.

Since the horrible events of September 11, the question must be asked, Is that advice still valid?

Yes. In fact, my advice is more important than ever.

This will surprise some people. After all, some will say, individuals who lost their job as a result of the September 11 attacks won't be able to pay their mortgage and consequently may lose their home.

The truth is that the risk of an unexpected job loss is one of the key reasons *to* carry a big mortgage, not a reason to avoid it.

I explained why in my second book, *The New Rules of Money*, and the people who have been following my advice are today protected from losing their homes—even if they've lost their jobs. You see, it's a myth that having a mortgage places you at risk of losing your house due to a job loss, and the people who have a big, long mortgage are not automatically in jeopardy today. Instead, in many cases it is the people who have been trying to own their homes outright who now are at greatest risk of losing them. Let me explain, with an example borrowed from *New Rules*.

First of all, losing your job has no direct impact on your mortgage. As long as you make your monthly payment, the bank cannot foreclose. This is important to understand, because in the 1920s and 1930s, banks could call loans at any time. In the Depression, millions of homeowners got such notices, and, without jobs or money, they failed to pay. The result: Millions of Americans lost their homes.

This can't happen anymore, because banks can't call your loan prematurely, like they once could.

Therefore, the only thing you need to worry about is your ability to pay the bank this month's payment—not the entire loan balance. Let's see how this applies in a real-life example.

## THE NUMBERS PROVE IT

Pat and Ed each earn $50,000 a year. Each has $20,000 in savings, and each buys a $120,000 house.

Pat wants to own his home outright, but he doesn't have the cash to do so. So he minimizes his mortgage by using his $20,000 as a down payment and opting for a 15-year loan at 7.5%. His monthly payment is $927, but only 67% of that payment is tax-deductible interest; the rest is principal. Therefore, Pat's after-tax cost for his mortgage is $742. And because he hates his mortgage, Pat sends an extra $100 to his lender every month. These extra payments are principal, not interest, and therefore provide no tax deduction.

Ed obtains a 30-year mortgage at 8% (30-year loans cost a bit more than 15-year loans, but, as you'll see, they're worth it). He puts down just 5%, or $6,000. Even though his mortgage balance is bigger than Pat's, his monthly payment is smaller (just $837), because he's financing it over a longer period (30 years instead of 15).

And because Ed's loan is for 30 years, 90% of his payment is interest, not just 67%, like Pat's. That means Ed's after-tax cost is just $586 a month—$156 less than what Pat pays!

Thanks to this lower payment, Ed is able to save that $156 each month. And while Pat sent an extra $100 to the mortgage lender every month, Ed keeps his cash in savings and investments.

Fast-forward several years. Ed and Pat are now both out of work, economic victims of the horrendous attack on America of September 11, 2001. Pat owes his bank $927 this month, but he hasn't got the money, because he's out of work. And because he's been sending all available cash to the lender every month, he has no savings, either. Result: He's about to lose his house.

Ed is in fine economic shape. Because he gave the bank only $6,000 at closing, he kept the other $14,000. Because his monthly payments were $156 less than Pat's, that's another several thousand in his kitty. Ditto with the extra $100 a month—Ed could have sent that cash to his mortgage company, like Pat did, but instead he added it to his savings.

Result: Ed has more than $20,000 in savings and investments. Now that he's out of work, he writes a check to his mortgage company for $837. He'll be able to do this for the next two years, which gives him a lot of time to get a new job. Pat, meanwhile, is moving in with his in-laws today.

Why doesn't Pat just tap into all the equity he's got in his house? He tried, but the bank turned him down for the loan. That's because home loans are based on your income, not on the value of the house. With no income, Pat doesn't qualify for a loan. (This explains why I told you in Chapter 2 not to rely on lines of credit for cash reserves.)

Ironic, no? Pat never wanted a mortgage and is now in financial jeopardy as a result. Ed is in much better shape.

# HOW TO MAKE THE MOST
# OF YOUR MORTGAGE

To protect yourself, your family, and your home, act immediately to:

1. Get as much cash out of your house as possible. Get a new loan if you don't already have one, refinance your current loan to a larger loan, or get a second mortgage.
2. Choose a 30-year loan, not a 15-year loan. The longer the term, the lower the payments and the higher the tax deduction.
3. If your current loan is more than 15 years old, refinance to replace it with a new 30-year loan. That's because payments on loans that old (or older) consist too much of principal, not interest. There's no tax break for payments of principal.
4. Never send extra cash to your lender. Place that cash into cash reserves, savings, and investments.
5. Never enroll in biweekly mortgage plans. They merely force you to send more money to the lender each year than is otherwise required. As a result, you lose access to more of your money, and you lose your tax deduction sooner than you otherwise would. Instead, make the minimum payment required, and place any excess cash you have into your savings and investments.

# MAKE SURE YOUR LOAN IS
# TAX-DEDUCTIBLE

Keep in mind that when you're refinancing, mortgage interest is tax-deductible only for the first $100,000 of new debt. This limit does not apply when you are obtaining the mortgage to purchase a home or using the money for home improvements. Say you have a current loan of $50,000 on a house worth $400,000. When you refinance, the interest on the first $150,000 is tax-deductible, even though the lender might be willing to loan you $320,000. In contrast, if you had borrowed $320,000 when purchasing that $400,000 house, the entire loan interest would be tax-deductible. This is why I encourage people to get as big a loan as possible when buying a home. As always, be sure to talk with your financial or tax advisor.

## WORRIED ABOUT MAKING THE NEW PAYMENTS?

If you fret that you won't be able to afford your new mortgage payment, just let your new investments help you.

After you get the cash out of your house, invest it. Then arrange for your new investments to send you a monthly check equal to your increased mortgage payments. In ordinary times, your investments should be able to produce as much income as your mortgage costs you. In troubled times, like we're facing today, your loan might be charging a rate higher than what you're currently earning. In my opinion, this is an acceptable trade-off, because the discrepancy will likely be only temporary, and in the meantime, you're able to keep control of your cash.

Think about it. Which would you rather have:

$200,000 in home equity but no cash in your bank and no mortgage payment
  *or*
$100,000 in home equity with $100,000 in your bank and an $800 monthly payment.

I'll take the second option every time and suggest you do, too.

If you're still not convinced that carrying a big, long mortgage is the safest way to approach home ownership, consider these points:

1. Mortgages do not affect home values. Your home will grow in value—or not—regardless of the mortgage. Thus, having lots of equity in the house is like stuffing money in a mattress—it doesn't earn any interest.

2. Worried that the house might fall in value after you get your loan? If that happens, consider yourself lucky (or smart!) for having already cashed out the equity. After all, you won't be able to tap into the equity after the house falls in value. So you had better do it now.

3. Mortgage loans offer you the cheapest money you'll ever borrow. Compare their tax-deductible rates to the nondeductible rates of credit cards.

---

**If you have equity in your house, take out a loan now, while you can, before you lose your job. As I explained earlier, people without an income can't get loans— regardless of their home's value.**

---

No matter what scenario you imagine—job loss, health problem, divorce or separation, unexpected expenses, falling market values, unstable economy, poor investment performance—you are *always* better off having cash and a mortgage than having a paid-for home and no cash. Period.

## CHAPTER 4

# Is Your Job Secure?

On September 10, most people felt that their jobs were secure. On September 11, they weren't so sure.

The hijackings and attacks on the Pentagon and the World Trade Center have proved that none of us have a secure job. Just look at the domino effect the attacks have had on the U.S. economy:

- Airlines laid off tens of thousands of workers; one airline went out of business permanently, firing 1,700 people.
- Boeing laid off 40,000 workers.
- In Las Vegas, the nation's no.1 convention city, all hotel construction projects were postponed or canceled. Thousands of construction workers were laid off.
- Reduced tourism caused at least four Broadway shows to cancel. Several touring shows were canceled or had their schedules reduced. Headline acts in Las Vegas and Atlantic City were canceled.
- Hotels around the country have laid off tens of thousands of workers, as conventions and meetings have been canceled or rescheduled.

- Television and radio networks lost millions of dollars in advertising revenue by airing 24-hour coverage of the crisis. Advertising agencies lost their commissions when the ads didn't air. Retailers, facing store closings and business losses, canceled their ad schedules, placing further pressure on the broadcasting and advertising industries.
- Hollywood lost millions of dollars as moviegoers stayed home. Several films about to be released were shelved because of their content, costing tens of millions more.
- The sports industry lost tens of millions of dollars when every professional and college athletic event was canceled for nearly two weeks. Everyone from parking garage attendants to food and souvenir vendors to referees was temporarily laid off.
- The stock market's shutdown cost financial firms as much as 2% of their annual earnings. Already in an economic slump, the brokerage industry is facing the loss of thousands of jobs.
- The real estate market was temporarily sidetracked. Few consumers went house-hunting in the week after the attack. Realtors throughout the U.S. reported little or no sales activity.
- Consumers held off purchasing big-ticket items, such as cars and big-screen televisions. Retail sales slumped.
- Homeowners delayed home repairs. Plumbers, electricians, architects, and builders saw substantially reduced business.
- Even the medical community isn't immune. Consumers delayed or canceled cosmetic and LASIK surgery, dental appointments, and other previously scheduled but nonurgent or optional procedures. Many private-practice professionals in the medical and dental fields have experienced a huge loss of income since September 11.

If someone had told you in August that a crop duster in Kansas would lose his job because of a coward's attack in New York, you wouldn't have believed him. Today, it's all too real. Consequently, we must examine job security in a new light.

Ask yourself: If your employer was unable to conduct business—if the company's stores were closed for a time, if the company's business clientele experienced financial difficulties or went out of business—how long would your employer be able and willing to keep you on the payroll?

## QUESTIONS EMPLOYEES MUST ASK

1. Ask your employer if they have business continuity coverage, also known as business overhead expense coverage. This insurance provides cash to your employer so the company can meet payroll and other expenses in the event that normal business operations are interrupted.

2. Ask your employer if they have a Phoenix plan. With a name based on Greek mythology—the Phoenix rose from the ashes—Phoenix plans are essentially disaster recovery plans. Does your company have a plan ready to be executed in the event that normal operations are interrupted? For example:

   a. What's the plan if no one can enter the office because of a fire or other emergency?

   b. What's the plan if the company's inventory is destroyed?

   c. What's the plan if the company's executives are killed, injured, or taken hostage—or merely away on vacation when a crisis strikes?

   d. Has the staff been properly trained in how to respond in each scenario? Does everyone know how to contact supervisors and coworkers if you hear on the late-night news that your building has caught fire?

As devastating as the events of September 11 were, from an economic perspective it would have been much worse had the many firms housed in and around the World Trade Center not been so well prepared. Ironically, this extensive preparation was thanks to the cowards themselves—the very criminals who bombed the WTC in 1993. At that time, about 300 businesses occupied the towers, and 26% of them never reopened. Why? Because they lost their data.

That lesson, along with the extensive worry about Y2K (remember that?!), led businesses to develop Phoenix systems like never before. As a result, after the September 11 attack, many companies' data were safe. They had taken care to store vital records off site, and many had arranged for "cold sites"—duplicate offices in New Jersey and Connecticut where their workers could resume business immediately. Thanks to such foresight, the financial community was able to resume operations within days of the attack.

Is your company so well prepared? Ask your boss today, and help him or her develop written operational procedures so that staff can fulfill each other's duties.

This is critical, because our biggest loss from the attacks was neither data nor money. It was the loss of more than 6,000 individuals, and the personal devastation this has wrought for their survivors remains uncalculable.

But the economic loss of those lives is calculable. Many executives and, in a few companies, nearly entire senior staffs, were lost. Did these companies have key-employee insurance coverage in place, so that business could continue without them? Does your employer have these policies or procedures in place?

I know this sounds crude and superficial in the face of the terrible personal losses so many of us experienced on September 11, and that the massive, unfathomable loss of life deserves all our attention. But that won't help the survivors. Out of respect and concern for the employees and customers of the American economy, we must tend to these matters, even though they pale beside the enormous personal losses of our loved ones.

**A**sk your employer today what plans they have for securing the company's viability.

## QUESTIONS EMPLOYERS MUST ANSWER

If you are a business owner or a corporate executive, take the following steps to help preserve your company's ability to survive a devastating disruption in operations:

1.  OBTAIN KEY-EMPLOYEE COVERAGE. If you lose an employee who is critical to the daily operations of your company, you could lose substantial revenue. Life and disability income insurance policies (antiquatedly called "key man" contracts by insurers) are intended to provide a company with the cash it would need to recruit a replacement and compensate the company for resulting financial losses. The cost of this insurance is comparable to that of other life and disability income policies (see Chapter 5).

2.  GET BUSINESS OVERHEAD EXPENSE COVERAGE. BOE coverage provides cash to your business so it can pay its bills, such as rent, utilities, and salaries, while the owner or key employee is unable to work. This coverage is particularly important for professionals in private practice, such as physicians, dentists, and attorneys. The receptionist can't drill teeth if the dentist-owner has broken a finger, and with no revenue from patients, the practice could quickly run out of money. If the rent is not paid, the landlord might evict the dentist. Certainly, the staff would leave for other jobs. When the dentist returns to work, there might not be a practice to return to! BOE coverage keeps the income flowing so the practice can hire a replacement dentist, let the staff retain their incomes, and keep business intact.

3. DEVELOP CASH MANAGEMENT STRATEGIES. In many cases, the problem isn't with your company—it's with your customer. To prevent problems that result from customers who can't pay their bills, as well as other interruptions in cash flow, develop solid cash management strategies. These include obtaining bank lines of credit, securing special financing terms with lenders and customers alike, and boosting cash reserves.

4. MAKE SURE YOU HAVE A STANDARD OPERATING PROCEDURES MANUAL. In most companies, everyone knows his or her own job description. But does anyone know anyone else's? It is vital that you document all policies and procedures for every member of the staff. This book, which should be updated annually, should be a step-by-step guide of how-to-do-what. It should include names and phone numbers of outside contacts as well as those of relevant staff.

5. CROSS-TRAIN YOUR STAFF. In most companies, people are expert at what they do—but no one else can do their job. Staff should be cross-trained to familiarize themselves with other corporate functions. No business should be dependent on the knowledge and skills of any one worker.

   In our company, we provide four-week paid sabbaticals to all staff upon their six-year anniversary. Because we know months in advance that we're going to lose a staffer for four weeks, we take advantage of the opportunity to train another staff member in his or her job. This enables the company's work to continue uninterrupted, promotes camaraderie among the staff, and improves client service.

6. REVISE ALL JOB DESCRIPTIONS. Have all members of your staff write their own job description, as though they were hiring their own replacement. These documents could serve as the basis for cross-training, development of operational procedures, and emergency recruitment.

7. KEEP DATA BACKUPS. Every business has data, be it on paper or stored in a computer. Paper can burn or be thrown away or have coffee spilled on it. Computers are certain to fail—disk drive manufacturers actually brag about their products' MTBF, or "mean time between failures"—so it's a foolhardy business owner who does not make frequent copies of all data produced in the business. In my firm, we back up our entire computer system three times a day. We also operate redundant, or mirrored, systems, which means that if the primary systems go down, the secondary systems take over instantaneously, with no loss of data and no interruption in service.

8. ARRANGE OFF-SITE STORAGE. Don't leave your backup files in your office. If the building is destroyed by water or fire, or simply cannot be entered, you must be able to retrieve your data from another location. Make certain that several key staff members have access to the off-site storage area as well (which, frankly, can simply be the basement of a staff member's house).

9. MAKE SURE EVERYONE HAS A STAFF DIRECTORY. All staff should carry with them at all times the home, cell, and pager numbers of all other staff members. You might need to reach people outside of normal business hours, if only to tell them that the office will be closed the next day due to snow. Make sure staff members safeguard this private information.

10. MAINTAIN A HOT LINE. All staff should know the phone number to call to learn of important company developments. Our staff know to call a certain number as early as 6:00 A.M. on days when a snowstorm might cause us to close our office or delay its opening. By leaving a recorded message on a hot line that all staff can call, you can communicate important information to the entire company very quickly.

11. INSTALL A PA SYSTEM. The offices should be equipped with a public address system, so that key personnel can instantly broadcast a message to everyone in the building.

12. DISTRIBUTE CRITICAL LISTS. Key executives and sales managers should keep at home paper lists of customers, vendors, and staff. In the event that access to corporate records or offices isn't possible, management can use these lists to contact key clients, customers, vendors, and suppliers to keep the business running. Make certain each member of your staff signs a confidentiality agreement to protect the information.

13. HIRE A SECURITY CONSULTANT. Your offices and personnel are vulnerable. Find out where and how by hiring a security consultant, and then implement the recommendations.

14. HIRE AN INFORMATION TECHNOLOGY CONSULTANT. Your computer systems are vulnerable, too, especially if you are connected to the Internet. An expert in the field of information technology can help you protect your systems—the lifeblood of your business—as well as maximize their effectiveness.

15. CONSIDER RESERVING A COLD SITE. If your business is run exclusively by in-house electronics, rather than by inventory, manufacturing, or service or at client sites, consider reserving space at a cold site facility. These are essentially entire office buildings equipped with all the technology you need to resume operations in the event that your primary offices cannot be used.

16. DISPERSE YOUR STAFF WHEN THEY TRAVEL. Don't let the entire staff fly on the same plane. When they attend conferences, have them stay in different hotels and on different floors of the same hotels (preferably low ones for easier and quicker egress).

17. DEVELOP AN EMERGENCY ADVERTISING PLAN. As soon as possible during a crisis, cancel all advertising, including

radio, television, print, and Internet ads and direct mail advertising, until all material can be reviewed for propriety relative to the current circumstances. Have all advertising contracts contain clauses that waive fees under such circumstances.

18. TRAIN, TRAIN, TRAIN. Make sure all staff know what to do in the event of an emergency. Drill regularly.

19. DEVELOP A COMMUNITY ACTION PLAN. Rather than affecting you directly, a crisis might affect your customers, vendors, or competitors—as well as consumers and the local community. Develop a plan that will enable you to quickly offer assistance to each of these groups, to help them through the crisis. Make certain that no staff member acts in any way that may be exploitative or even appear so.

20. DEVELOP YOUR EXIT STRATEGY. At some point, every business owner will die, retire, or sell the business. Develop an exit strategy now, one that considers the possibility that you might die sooner than expected or become disabled. (This is especially important if you have partners. If you fail to plan and your partner dies, you don't inherit his or her share of the business. Instead, the deceased's spouse or kids become your new partner!) Make certain that your plan takes into consideration your staff and your customers, for the opportunity to operate a business in America also has its obligations.

---

**I**f you are a business owner or corporate executive, assemble your key staff and begin to implement these strategies today.

---

## CHAPTER 5

# Make Sure Your Family Is Financially Protected

L IFE IS FULL OF RISKS. Some are predictable, and some—as we learned on September 11—aren't.

In this chapter, I'll tell you what you need to do <u>right now</u> to protect your family from sudden, catastrophic financial ruin.

There are several ways you can protect yourself financially from the risks inherent in everyday life:

**AVOID THE RISK:** You can simply avoid the risky activity. Problem solved. Unfortunately, this is not realistic or practical in many cases.

**REDUCE THE RISK:** You can reduce the likelihood of a loss, as well as the extent of it, by reducing your exposure to the risk. For example, wearing a seat belt reduces the risk of injury when riding in a car. What changes in your habits can you adopt that can reduce your risk of incurring a financial loss?

DIVERSIFY THE RISK: Own many types of investments, not just one. Have staff and family travel to distant events in different cars, planes, and trains. Keep copies of important documents in multiple locations, and back up computer disks and hard drives regularly.

TRANSFER THE RISK: Find someone willing to assume the risks that you cannot avoid, reduce, or diversify. The most common and practical way to transfer risk is through insurance, and that's what we're going to explore in this chapter.

## HEALTH INSURANCE: A PRIMER

You don't need me to tell you that you need health insurance for yourself and your family. You also don't need me to tell you that health insurance is expensive, complicated, and confusing. Here's a basic primer on the subject.

### The Five Types of Coverage

You can choose from five types of health insurance coverage:

HOSPITAL INSURANCE: This type of policy covers such costs as room and board, lab and nursing services, medication, and supplies.

SURGICAL INSURANCE: This covers the services of surgeons and anesthesiologists.

MEDICAL INSURANCE: This pays for doctor visits and out-patient costs.

MAJOR MEDICAL INSURANCE: This type of policy pays the cost of huge medical bills—often up to $1 million—but only after you pay the initial cost (called the "deductible"). Even after you do that, these policies often require that you pay 20% to 30% of the bill, up to a certain amount. For example, a major medical policy might have a $2,000 deductible and an 80/20 co-insurance clause up to $10,000. This means you'll pay the first $2,000 of any bill, plus 20% of the next $8,000. All other covered charges will be paid by the insurance company.

COMPREHENSIVE MAJOR MEDICAL INSURANCE: These policies are a combination of the other four and feature much lower deductibles (such as $200 instead of $2,000). Because of this, these policies cost more than the others.

## The Four Types of Insurance Providers

As if the various types of insurance aren't confusing enough, there are four types of organizations that offer coverage:

BLUE CROSS/BLUE SHIELD: Blue Cross contracts with doctors and hospitals, who agree to charge certain fees. "Participating" doctors and hospitals will accept payment from the Blues as full payment; if you use "nonparticipating" doctors and hospitals, the fees will be higher, and you'll be required to pay the excess.

PRIVATE INSURANCE COMPANIES: All doctors and hospitals are, essentially, nonparticipating—but you get to choose your own. Because the resulting costs are higher, these policies often have more exclusions, and they limit the amount they'll pay for each medical procedure. If you incur higher costs, you will be required to pay them.

PREFERRED PROVIDER ORGANIZATIONS: PPOs have agreements with certain doctors and hospitals, similar to the Blues. They usually cover 100% of most charges, provided that the insured first visits one of the PPO's primary care physicians (who are internists or family practitioners). If the insured visits an "out-of-network" doctor or is not referred to an "in-network" specialist by the primary care physician, the policy will not pay 100% of the fees charged. There usually is a minimum payment for office calls and a deductible when visiting a hospital's emergency room as well.

HEALTH MAINTENANCE ORGANIZATIONS: Unlike insurance companies that reimburse medical providers for services rendered, you *prepay* HMOs. Later, when you need medical services, you and the members of your household receive them at no charge (other than small fees for office visits).

This business model gives HMOs a built-in incentive to keep clients healthy. As a result, supposedly, they focus on preventive care; for example, HMOs usually pay for physical examinations, something other health insurance policies don't cover.

However, since the HMO generates no revenue when a member receives medical attention, some critics believe the quality of care suffers. For example, with the Blues, PPOs, and private insurers, you are permitted to select your own doctor (although in many cases you must select from a list of participating physicians). With HMOs, the insured sees whoever is available and might not see the same doctor twice.

Furthermore, HMOs usually require patients to see a general practitioner before seeing a specialist. The general practitioner is supposed to refer the patient to a specialist, but some GPs have been known to perform medical procedures that should be done by a specialist, again as a way to save money for the HMO.

---

**L**ook at your current health insurance policy today and compare it to the alternatives discussed here. If you don't think your policy is best, start shopping immediately. If your policy is provided to you at work, talk with your human resources department to learn what options are available to you.

---

## The Two Types of Policies To Avoid

Some policies are meant to be sold, not bought. Two types to avoid:

ACCIDENT INSURANCE: These policies pay a specific dollar amount for every day a patient stays in a hospital—provided he or she is there because of an injury, not illness. These policies essentially are a bet that you won't ever be sick enough to require medical treatment—a foolish bet.

DREAD DISEASE INSURANCE: This type of policy pays only if a patient contracts a specific disease, such as cancer. Again, it's a silly bet.

---

**Avoid accident and dread disease insurance, and if you have such policies, cancel them in favor of more comprehensive policies (after confirming that you qualify for them). You want insurance that will pay because you incur costs, not because you incur costs for certain reasons.**

---

## How to Evaluate Your Health Insurance Policy

The following questions and tips will help you identify the strengths and weaknesses of the medical insurance coverage you have or are considering buying. For the answers to these questions, look in your policy documents, contact the agent who sold you the policy, or, if your employer provides the policy, contact your human resources department.

1. WHAT IS THE DOLLAR AMOUNT OF THE DEDUCTIBLE? Health insurance is supposed to protect you from the high

costs of medical care. The less you pay for medical services, the higher the cost of the policy.

---

**O**ne of the best ways to reduce the cost is to increase the deductible. Increase your deductible by agreeing to pay the first $1,000 (or even more). The cost of the policy will drop significantly.

---

And if that unexpected medical need arises? Well, that's what your cash reserves are for!

2. DO YOU PAY YOUR DEDUCTIBLE ONCE PER YEAR OR PER ILL-NESS? Preferably, you pay your deductible only once per year, not once per illness.

3. WHAT PERCENTAGE OF COVERED MEDICAL EXPENSES DOES YOUR POLICY PAY? If your policy pays 100% of costs, the monthly premium will be prohibitively expensive. If it pays only 50% of the charges, you could be hit with a huge medical bill unexpectedly. Look for a policy that strikes an acceptable balance between the two.

4. DOES YOUR POLICY INCLUDE A CO-INSURANCE CAP OR "STOP LOSS" LIMIT? It should. A co-insurance cap means you pay only a share of medical expenses, up to a certain limit (often $5,000 or $10,000). After you pay that limit, the policy pays all other covered costs. Decide how much you are prepared to pay in total annual expenses. $5,000? $25,000? More? Less? Seek a policy that limits your exposure to that amount.

5. WHAT IS THE MAXIMUM DOLLAR AMOUNT YOUR POLICY WILL PAY DURING YOUR LIFETIME? Ideally, your policy will not have any limit, but most do. Any limit below $1 million is not acceptable.

6. WHAT IS THE EMERGENCY ROOM DEDUCTIBLE? Often, the deductible is $50 or more—to discourage visits to the ER. If

you go to the ER for a nonemergency, your deductible may be even higher unless you notify your primary care physician before you arrive.

7. HOW SOON AFTER YOU ARE ADMITTED TO THE ER MUST YOU NOTIFY YOUR DOCTOR? If you fail to act within the required period, your expenses might not be covered. See what your policy's requirements are, and decide if they are reasonable. And until you get a better policy, make sure you comply with this requirement.

8. DOES YOUR POLICY LIMIT COVERAGE FOR CERTAIN CHARGES, SUCH AS HOSPITAL ROOM AND BOARD? If it does, check with area hospitals to see if this limit will cover the cost. Often, insurers insert an "internal limit" on such costs, which results in your paying more than what you'd expect based on the co-payment percentage (see question 3). Also, many policies do not pay the costs of a private room, so explore those costs, too, and decide if you're willing to pay the difference *before* you ask for or agree to a private room.

9. WHAT IS THE MAXIMUM NUMBER OF DAYS YOUR HOSPITAL STAY WILL BE COVERED FOR A SINGLE ILLNESS OR INJURY? This is another type of internal limit. Not all policies have these limits, but if yours does, you probably need a second policy to pick up costs after your present one stops providing benefits.

## Five Ways to Lose Your Employer-Provided Health Insurance

Think you're safe because you have a good medical policy?
Think again. You could lose your coverage if:

1. You quit your job.
2. You get fired.
3. You have a preexisting condition not covered by your new employer.

4. You divorce your spouse, who pays the insurance premiums.
5. Your spouse, who pays the insurance premiums, dies.

If you lose employer-provided health insurance, ask your human resources office about COBRA coverage. COBRA is a law that in many cases enables you or a family member to maintain health insurance coverage for 18 to 36 months after you lose your employer-provided insurance. You'll have to pay for COBRA coverage, which is not cheap, and it expires in a relatively short period, so you should immediately seek alternative insurance.

## LIFE INSURANCE: CUT IN HALF AND DROP A ZERO

September 11 gave us a hard lesson on how unpredictable life can be. After the initial wave of shock and sadness passed, I found myself muttering, "I hope the victims had life insurance."

That might seem like a ridiculous, even callous, comment. But it comes from my heart, for too often people have sought our help only *after* finding themselves in severe financial jeopardy as a result of a family member's death.

Having worked with hundreds of such cases, I can tell you this: If you think losing a loved one is the worst thing that could happen to you, you're wrong. The worst thing that can happen to you is losing a loved one and *then* discovering that as a result, your children can't go to college or you can't keep your home. Dealing with bill collectors while dealing with grief is far worse than dealing with grief alone.

I don't know how many of the victims of the September 11 attack had life insurance. Most of the victims were employed and, being white-collar workers or military personnel, carried some amount of life insurance (often, one or two times their salary) provided by their employers. And America has rallied to aid their families as well, with hundreds of millions of dollars already donated to relief efforts. No doubt, some of this money will find its way to the victims' families.

But you can't be so sure that when you die, teenagers half a continent away will stage a carwash to aid your family, or that the television networks will broadcast a benefit concert featuring top musicians from the U.S. and England to raise money for your kids, or that someone will write a book and donate the profits to your spouse. No, I regret to say, when you die, your family might get a few casseroles from well-meaning neighbors, but that's about it.

## So ask yourself: How much life insurance do you have?

My bet: Not enough.

If you don't believe me, try the following simple test I've created for you.

## Cut in Half and Drop a Zero

I've devised this admittedly too simple formula so you can easily see if the amount of insurance you have is enough to protect your family. Let's say you have $300,000 in life insurance.

Step one: Cut that number in half. This reduces the figure to $150,000.

Step two: Drop a zero. Thus reduces the $150,000 to $15,000.

Voilà!

You have the answer: A $300,000 life insurance policy will generate $15,000 a year in income for your surviving family. That's *pre-tax* income, by the way. Meaning that your $300,000 policy will provide your family with about $1,000 a month to support themselves.

Do you still think you have a lot of life insurance?

Think about this very carefully. Upon your death, your family will not use the insurance proceeds to pay off the mortgage—not because they've read Chapter 3 but because of something much easier to understand: If they pay off the mortgage, they'll have no money left. How would they pay for food, let alone college?

Instead, they'll set the money aside to produce an income. And assuming a 5% annual return—which is what my formula produces—a $300,000 policy will produce a $15,000 annual income. Pre-tax.

No question about it: The vast majority of Americans are woefully underinsured.

This is easy to understand. First of all, Americans love to hate insurance companies and their salespeople. You think they're just trying to make a sale so they can earn their commission. You also think you don't need life insurance, because you're not going to die young. You figure you won't die until you're in your 70s, 80s, or 90s—heck, my grandmother lived to 101!—and by then, your kids won't be financially dependent on you. Besides, by then, you and your spouse will have pensions plus plenty of money in investments, making life insurance unnecessary. No doubt about it: Your long life span—you know, the one you're certain to enjoy—will give you plenty of time to accrue all those pension benefits and fat investment holdings, and by the time you die, your spouse and kids will be so well established that money will not be a problem.

Yup, it's a great plan you have there. It's also probably what many of the victims of September 11 thought.

By the way, the average wife in America becomes a widow at age 54.

You might want to rethink your assumptions.

How much life insurance to own is a topic hotly debated in financial circles. Simple formulas—including the one I have shared with you—never suffice, but they can help focus the conversation.

**T**he first question to ask yourself is: If you died today, who would suffer financially?

Note the word *financially*. Insurance is an economic issue, not an emotional one. We know that your death would be a tragedy for your loved ones, but we're talking here about finances.

It's quite possible that no one would suffer financially as a result of your death.

For example, if you're an adult living independently with no spouse, children, other family members, or others who are dependent on you for financial support, you don't need any life insurance.

But if you're married, if you have young children, if you send money monthly to help support your parents or other relatives, or if others depend on you for financial aid, you have a responsibility to make sure that your death will not impose a financial burden on them or place them in financial jeopardy.

The amount of insurance you need is determined by a variety of factors:

- your age,
- your health,
- your income,
- your expenses,
- the number and circumstances of family members financially dependent on you,
- your attitude regarding the extent of protection you wish to provide.

That last point is worth elaboration. Say you're 35 years old, earn $50,000 a year, are married, and have three kids under age 10 and your spouse is a stay-at-home parent. My cut-in-half-and-drop-a-zero formula suggests that you'd need $1 million in life insurance, so that upon your death, your spouse could replace your salary.

But this assumes two important points: that your spouse will need that $50,000 income for the remainder of his or her life and that your spouse will never deplete the $1 million you leave.

Is this really your intention—or even necessary? All that's necessary, perhaps, is to provide your surviving spouse with income for just a few years, enough time for him or her to

- Get the kids into college.
- Get a job.
- Remarry.

You must decide how much financial support you want to leave your family and how long you want that support to be provided. Clearly, the less income you want them to receive, and the less time you want them to receive it, the less insurance you need to buy.

I've counseled thousands of people on this subject, and have seen many different attitudes and opinions. Some people want to make certain that their spouse is financially secure for the spouse's expected lifetime. Others fully expect their spouse to get a job and remarry, and therefore want to provide only enough support to help the spouse make that transition.

How you feel about this subject affects whether you buy a multimillion-dollar policy or one that pays only $100,000. My personal view on this is not important, because I'm not married to your spouse, and your kids aren't my own. But what I am adamant about is this: Make sure that the insurance amount you have is the result of a deliberate, conscious decision, and not simply a default amount.

Too often, when people die, the only insurance they leave behind is the policy they had at work. Or it's a small policy they bought years ago. As a result, whether it was their intention or not, their surviving spouse is forced to return to the workplace, or take a second job, and the kids can't afford to attend college—

not because of some "grand plan" but simply because the deceased didn't gave it enough (any?) thought.

After all, $300,000 sounds like plenty of insurance! Yet, as you've seen, this figure produces a remarkably small amount of income.

And that's too bad—because you probably don't have even $300,000 in coverage. According to the American Council of Life Insurers, the average American household has only $165,800 in life insurance. That's enough, based on my quickie formula, to produce just $8,290 a year in income.

Shame on you if you die and leave your family financially destitute because you didn't buy insurance even though you could have. "I can't afford it" doesn't work, because you subscribe to cable TV, own a VCR, and maybe have a video camera, too. If you can afford those things, you can afford to buy insurance that will protect your loved ones.

---

**In fact, the only valid reason for not owning life insurance is a medical condition that makes you uninsurable. If you are insurable, apply for life insurance today—before an accident, injury, or time makes you uninsurable.**

---

Now that you've decided to buy (more) insurance, you've got to decide what kind: temporary or permanent. Let's examine each one.

## Temporary Insurance

Better known as "term life," temporary insurance has two features: the amount of the death benefit and the price of the policy. You pay for the policy, and when you die, the insurance company pays the death benefit to your survivors. When you buy the policy, you tell the insurance company who you want to receive the insurance proceeds; these people are called the *beneficiaries*.

Term is considered "temporary" because it covers you only for one year. When you buy term insurance, you're betting you're going to die within 12 months; the insurer is betting you won't. If you don't die, your money is gone (the insurance company keeps it), and you pay for another year's coverage. You do this every year until . . . well, until you win the bet!

## The Three Kinds of Term Insurance

You can choose from three kinds of term insurance:

ANNUAL RENEWABLE TERM: Each year the cost rises, because each year you become more likely to die. ART costs very little when you're young: A 30-year-old nonsmoking woman in excellent health can buy a $500,000 policy for as little as $180, while a 70-year-old woman might spend thousands.

LEVEL TERM: This policy's cost does not grow annually, like ART. Instead, the cost remains the same for 5, 10, or 20 years. It's more expensive than ART in the beginning but is cheaper overall, and that's why we usually recommend level term for our clients instead of ART.

DECREASING TERM: This is the opposite of ART. Instead of increasing the cost each year, this policy decreases the death benefit. Since most people want their heirs to receive the same amount of insurance no matter when they die, we never recommend it.

*The Hidden Bad Deal of Decreasing Term:* The most common form of decreasing term is called "mortgage life." It's often pitched to new homeowners, and it's a bad deal.

Here's the scenario: A young couple stretches to buy their new home, and they fret that if anything happens to one of them, the other will not be able to afford the mortgage payments. So, for low annual premiums that never increase, they each buy a policy with a death benefit equal to the outstanding mortgage balance.

What's the problem?

With each monthly payment, the mortgage balance declines, and the death benefit declines with it.

Think about it. This is not mortgage insurance, because they are not insuring the *mortgage*—they are insuring their *lives*. But by calling it "mortgage" insurance, companies often get away with charging substantially more than if they just called it "decreasing term" coverage.

Mortgage policies have two other problems:

- Even though the cost of living rises over time, the insurance coverage goes down.
- If one spouse dies, the insurance company writes a check to the mortgage lender; the surviving spouse never sees the money, even though he or she might need it for other, more pressing reasons. As we discussed in Chapter 3, paying off the mortgage is not necessarily the best use of insurance proceeds.

This is why you're better off buying ART or level term rather than decreasing term (assuming that term is the way to go—see next section), and why you should avoid mortgage life insurance.

## Permanent Insurance

Instead of buying insurance that lasts only for a short time (even 20 years is a short time compared to your life expectancy), it can make economic sense to buy a policy that lasts your entire life.

People choose "permanent" coverage when they believe their need for insurance will not go away. For example, if the only reason you're buying insurance is to make sure your 12-year-old can go to college, then a 10-year level term policy would be sufficient, because by the time the decade is up, the child will have graduated and the insurance will no longer be needed.

What if you want to make certain that your spouse will be financially protected for his or her lifetime, no matter when you die? Term insurance might not suffice, because it could expire while you're still alive.

This isn't mere conjecture; less than 5% of all term policies ever pay a claim. The rest expire—or policy owners cancel them—before the insureds die.

---

**A**sk yourself: How long do you want to keep the policy? The longer you plan to keep the coverage, the more cost-effective permanent insurance will be over your lifetime.

---

Note those last three words: "over your lifetime." It's important to understand that permanent insurance is designed to be economically viable for your remaining lifetime, not just for now (or some short period). This means that in the beginning, permanent coverage is much more expensive than term. Why pay this extra cost? Because 20, 30, 40 years from now, you'll be glad you did.

This can be small consolation for the young parents of small children who are struggling to make ends meet. They need cost-effective coverage today, not something that's expensive today but will be cost-effective decades from now.

This is why the decision regarding what type of insurance to buy—term versus permanent—is so complex, and why nothing can replace the advice of a professional financial planner. You must balance your need for insurance against your need to minimize expenses (which enables you to free up cash that you can invest for your future). This balancing act is not always clear-cut or easy. A good advisor can help.

## *The Three Kinds of Permanent Insurance*

When you meet with your advisor, you'll discover that there are three types of permanent insurance policies:

WHOLE LIFE: Unlike term insurance, which charges you on a pay-as-you-go basis, with costs tied to your current age (and life expectancy), whole life policies charge you the same price every year, no matter how old you get. They manage this by over-charging you in the early years (when you're relatively young) and undercharging you in later years (when you're relatively older). This is what makes whole life expensive in the short term (compared to term insurance) but economically viable in the long term.

Let's talk about that "overcharging" thing, because it's the key to the complexity—and viability—of permanent insurance. Since, in the early years, you're paying more for the policy than it really costs, what's the insurance company doing with the excess cash you've given them?

They invest it.

This is why permanent life insurance is so much more compli-cated than term life. With a term contract, there are only two fea-tures: what you pay to own it and what they pay upon your death. Permanent life has a third feature: the interest rate you earn on the excess cash you give them in the early years.

These interest earnings—which are put into an *accumulation account*—are critical, because the higher the interest, the lower the cost of your policy. And you can withdraw the money in the accumulation account any time you want. Because there is no such account in a term policy, you never have anything in it to withdraw.

In a whole life contract, everything is guaranteed: the cost of the policy, the death benefit, the interest rate the policy earns, and the future value of the accumulation account. And since everything is guaranteed, the guarantees are quite conservative. The insurance company is making only those promises it's sure it can fulfill—that it won't increase your costs, that it will pay the promised death benefit, and that the accumulation account will grow to certain values.

Consequently, whole life contracts charge high premiums—so that later, the company won't wish it was charging more—and promise that the future value of the accumulation account will be rather low.

The good news is you know what you're getting. The bad news is you're not getting much. Which takes us to . . .

UNIVERSAL LIFE: These policies invest your excess cash, just as whole life policies do, but unlike whole life, which credits cash with a low but predictable interest rate, universal life policies try to earn higher returns. When they succeed, they credit you with the higher earnings. Since they assume that they will be successful, they charge you less than whole life policies.

The problem, of course, is that they don't always succeed at earning more. When they fail to earn their predicted returns—and in the past 25 years, they have failed lots of times—the value of the accumulation account isn't as high as it's supposed to be. And you discover there's less available to withdraw. Even worse, the lower accumulation forces the insurance company to increase the amount you must pay to keep the policy in force. If you don't pay the higher amount, your policy could be canceled.

If you want to be certain that your premium will never rise, choose whole life. If you want to pay less now, choose universal life, but be aware that you may have to pay a higher amount later if current assumptions about future interest rates prove to be wrong.

And if you *really* want to gamble with your life insurance, choose . . .

VARIABLE LIFE: This type of policy allows you to invest your excess cash into mutual funds. The good news is that your accumulation account may grow more quickly than it would in either a whole life or a universal life policy. The bad news is that it might not grow at all, because in a variable life policy, there are *no* guarantees. If the mutual fund decreases in value, so does your accumulation account. In fact, if you choose a stock fund and the stock market drops—like it's done over the past 18 months—your accumulation account could be wiped out and your policy could be canceled for lack of funds *just when you need it most*. I am not a fan of variable life policies, and it is extremely rare for us to recommend them to our clients.

## How to Comparison Shop for Permanent Life Insurance

It's easy to compare permanent life policies, because they all have the same three variables: the death benefit, the premium, and the assumed interest rate that is used to grow the accumulation account. All you have to do when comparing one permanent life proposal to another is make sure that two of the three variables are the same. Then you can shop for the third variable. The best buy is the proposal that produces the best answer, whether that's the highest death benefit, the lowest premium, or the most cash value as projected in the 20th, 30th, or 40th year. That's all there is to it.

Search for whichever variable is most important to you. Some people want the most death benefit they can afford. Others want to keep their premium within a certain budget, and still others want to build a certain value in their accumulation account by a certain date.

Regardless of which variable you shop for, it is vital that the assumed interest rate in each proposal be identical—and realistic. Don't let one proposal show a 5% rate while another displays 5.5%. And make sure the rate they use is reasonable.

### Don't Let the Accumulation Account Grow Too Much

I also recommend that you design your policy so that the amount you pay is sufficient to keep the policy in force but does not let the accumulation account grow to a huge sum.

Why not? Because you'll never see that money.

The truth is that the accumulation account is a dirty little secret of the insurance industry. Say you own a $500,000 policy in which the accumulation account contains $50,000. Watch what happens:

- If you die, your heirs get $500,000—not $550,000. Thus, the fact that your accumulation account has fifty grand in it is irrelevant.
- If you withdraw that $50,000 during your lifetime—which you're allowed to do tax free under current law—your heirs will receive upon your death only $450,000, not the $500,000 you think your policy provides. Thus, you aren't "borrowing" the money from your policy's accumulation account—you're stealing it from your heirs!

## Which Type of Insurance Is Best?

Like so many other areas of personal finance, each type of insurance offers strengths and weaknesses. Which type to buy depends on your circumstances. Nothing can replace the personal advice provided by your financial planner or insurance agent.

For most of us, though, it's not a question of one or the other, for most people have more than one need for insurance. Term might be best to get the kids through college, while permanent is best to protect your spouse. This is why many people obtain two policies, one temporary and one permanent.

## The Cheapest Way to Buy Insurance on Children

Many parents buy life insurance policies on the lives of their young children. What an incredible waste of money.

It's much cheaper to add an optional "child rider" onto your own policy than to obtain a separate policy for the child. Such riders cost as little as $5 for $1,000 in coverage, meaning a $50 annual cost is all it would take to cover funeral expenses.

There's no reason to buy more coverage than that, unless your school age children happen to be earning a living. Remember, insurance is needed only when there is a **financial** loss. And although no one can imagine anything worse than the loss of a child, in most cases such a loss is not a financial one.

## The Life Insurance You Already Own Has Been Eroded by Inflation

The insurance you have might have been enough when you bought it long ago, but it's quite possible that inflation has severely eroded its value.

You'd be amazed how often I come across people who still have the $10,000 policies they bought 30 or 40 years ago. Don't believe me? Go ask your parents. I bet they have one.

Even though you're *sure* you have enough insurance, if you haven't bought a policy in many years, you probably don't.

If that's the case, you'll have to buy a new insurance policy, since most policies don't let you increase the coverage. You have a choice: You can keep your current policy and add a new one to supplement it, or you can replace the current policy with one that does provide sufficient coverage.

Which way to go depends on many factors:

- your age,
- how long you have owned the current policy,
- the cost of the policy,
- the current policy's death benefit,
- the current policy's cash value, if any,
- the amount of additional coverage you need,
- your health.

Because everyone's situation is different, you need to obtain the advice of a financial advisor or insurance agent to determine which course of action is best for you.

## You're Relying Too Much on Employer-Provided Coverage

Does your employer offer you life insurance as a benefit? Many companies do, and a policy equal to once or twice your salary is common. Free is free, so if your boss offers you insurance as a free benefit, fine. But before you decide to limit your coverage to this, realize that you are covered only while you have your job. If you quit or get fired, you lose the coverage. Also, employers can cancel the benefit at any time, leaving you with no protection.

Sometimes employers invite their workers to buy additional coverage at the worker's cost. If your employer gives you this option, it's usually best to reject the offer and buy the additional coverage you need independently.

Why? Because group-based policies can cost you substantially more than an individual policy. That's because group insurers must accept all people in the group, even those whose health is substandard. Since people who can't get coverage elsewhere are the quickest to accept group policies, claims rates are higher and therefore so are the costs.

If you are in good health, talk with your insurance agent or financial advisor to see if an individual policy would be better for you than the group policy. Chances are, it will be.

## Buy Few, Not Many, Life Insurance Policies

If you decide that you need $500,000 in life insurance, buy one policy for $500,000, not five policies of $100,000 each. If you decide that you need a combination of term and permanent, buy one, not several, of each.

Every policy charges fees that are unrelated to the amount of coverage. If you buy two policies instead of one, you pay these base costs twice instead of once. Therefore, you'll save money by buying fewer policies rather than many.

---

**I**f you already have many older policies, see if you can exchange them for fewer, newer ones.

---

## One Dumb Feature to Avoid

Since September 11, some life insurance agents have been touting the advantages of a rider called an "accidental death benefit," sometimes called "double indemnity."

This rider says that if your death is caused by an accident, your heirs will receive additional money—depending on the rider, as much as twice the normal death benefit.

It's an absurd option, because death is death: Dying in a bus accident—or, God forbid, a horrific attack such as occurred on September 11—instead of dying from cancer is not going to change your family's financial need. Therefore, get the coverage you need and skip this rider. Ditto for "cancer life" and similar policies that pay only if you die from certain causes.

Remember: Life insurance should cover death itself, not merely certain causes of death.

## Beware Paralysis of Analysis

I've given you a lot to digest about life insurance policies, probably more than you needed and certainly more than you wanted. Sometimes, all this education can cause people to develop what advisors call "paralysis of analysis"—a malady whereby clients do nothing while they evaluate their choices.

Don't let yourself get stuck on the details. This can be dangerous, because in the meantime, you don't have the life insurance coverage your family needs. Remember this: No matter which type of policy you choose, a bad policy that you own is better than a good policy that you don't own.

---

**G**o get life insurance *right now*. You can always change it later. After all, *right now* you are alive and well. And September 11 showed all of us that we cannot make that statement about tomorrow with any certainty.

---

## DISABILITY INCOME PROTECTION: YOU'RE THE OTHER GUY

If our conversation about life insurance hasn't given you lots to think about, this next one will.

The attack on America, which killed so very many people, also injured many, many people. I bet you think this kind of bad stuff only happens to the other guy. Well, to the other guy, you're the other guy. None of the many people injured in the attack thought they might become disabled that day. Like you, they thought it would happen to the other guy.

And yet, only 15% of U.S. workers have disability income (DI) protection, and the vast majority of those who do rely on employer-provided policies—a huge error that I'll explain in a moment.

Every homeowner in the country has fire insurance, even though the odds that your house will burn down are 1 in 1,200. In contrast, only 1 in 7 workers has DI coverage, even though the odds that you'll suffer a disability before age 65, one that lasts 90 days or more, is an incredible 1 in 8.

Statistics have been kept for such a long time that actuaries can now predict with remarkable accuracy how likely you are to become disabled prior to age 65. For example, as I show in *The Truth About Money*, of any five people who are age 45, it is 95%

certain that at least one will suffer a long-term disability. It would be foolish to bet against those odds, yet that's what you're doing if you do not have DI protection.

Ironically, technological, medical, and industrial advances have actually increased the likelihood that you'll become disabled one day. That's because our modern way of life has reduced your risk of death. Since 1960, the frequency of death from the four leading causes—hypertension, heart disease, cerebrovascular illness, and diabetes—has decreased 32%, while the frequency of disability from these conditions has increased 55%.

I call this the Air Bag Phenomenon. Thanks to the innovation of air bags, many people caught in auto accidents go to the emergency room instead of the morgue. Indeed, a study by the University of Pittsburgh showed that people protected by airbags who were involved in high-speed, head-on collisions often suffered injuries caused by the *air bag,* not the collision. These injuries included burns, loss of hearing and vision, and broken bones. Similar findings were reported by the University of Florida.

So the good news is that you're less likely to die in an auto accident. The bad news is that you're more likely to be injured.

Our medical advances go far beyond the highway. Throughout the United States, emergency medical technicians are trained to apply pacemakers at the scene. Got a bad colon? We'll cut it out. Clogged arteries? A quadruple bypass will put you back on your feet in weeks. High cholesterol? Take a pill.

Although modern medicine can prolong your life and improve its quality, this doesn't mean you'll never miss a day of work. Quite the contrary. The *Journal of the American Medical Association* published a study of more than 2,000 severely ill patients from five medical centers around the country that showed that nearly one-third of these patients' families lost most of their life savings as a result of the patient's illness. Although 96% of the patients had some form of medical insurance, 31% still lost their savings.

"Home care and disability costs may now be more devastating to patients and their families than the costs incurred in the hospital," the researchers wrote. These expenses include the following unreimbursed costs:

- home care,
- health aides,
- special transportation,
- related medical costs.

In addition, 29% of the families studied lost a major source of income, either because the patient no longer could work or because another family member had to quit a job to care for the patient.

All this makes perfect sense. After all, just because you slip on the ice and break your leg doesn't mean you can skip your mortgage payment or eat food for free. Your bills continue even if your income doesn't.

---

**A**re you willing to let financial devastation hit your family merely because of an accident or injury? You need to buy disability income insurance today.

---

## DI Coverage Isn't Cheap

Annual DI premiums can be 1% to 3% of your annual salary. That's why many people refuse to buy this insurance. "Too much money!" they say.

But if you can't afford the premium, how will you be able to afford the loss of income that results from being disabled?

You have to understand that DI coverage is expensive because the company knows there is a high likelihood that you will file a claim. The more that policyholders file claims, the more insurance companies must charge. Therefore, when a company tells you that the cost of coverage is high, the company is really telling you how important it is that you buy the protection.

There's another reason DI is so expensive: It costs much more to support a living person who is disabled than it does to pay the survivors of someone who has died.

Consider a 40-year-old who earns $75,000 a year and owns a $500,000 life insurance policy as well as a DI policy that pays 60% of pay to age 65. If she dies, the insurance company must pay $500,000. If she is disabled, the insurer would pay $45,000 per year for 30 years—a total of $1,350,000.

If you think the cost of DI coverage is expensive, I hope you never have to experience the cost of trying to live without it when you need it.

### Never Buy a Cheap DI Policy

The cheaper a DI policy, the less likely it will pay a claim, and if a claim is paid, the less it will pay. This is very different from life insurance, where buying the least expensive policy often is a very smart strategy.

With life insurance, no one debates whether the insured has died, but with DI, the debate is huge. Is the insured truly disabled? Says who? Does the disability meet the definition in the contract, and who makes that decision—your doctor or the insurance company's doctor?

Indeed, how disability is defined is perhaps the most important factor affecting the cost (and value) of the policy. That's why you must not buy a policy whose main attraction is a low price. Cheap policies have limited definitions, making it difficult to qualify for payments. More expensive policies have more liberal definitions.

My favorite example is a surgeon who loses a finger. Is he disabled? Under a standard contract, no, because the doctor can teach or consult, and his income might not suffer even though he can't perform surgery anymore.

But better contracts would agree that he's disabled because he can't perform the duties of "his own occupation" rather than "any" occupation. Amazing what impact a few words in a multi-page insurance contract can have.

And what if you can work part-time? Many standard policies deny claims unless you're unable to work at all. Better contracts pay partial benefits for partial income losses. (Now you know why the Social Security Administration, which uses a "totally disabled" definition, denies more than 90% of claims filed.)

### Don't Rely on Group DI Coverage

If you have DI coverage, it's probably because you get it free as an employee benefit. I mentioned earlier that this is a big problem. Let me now tell you why.

Group DI has the same drawbacks as group life insurance (which I discussed earlier) and presents still another problem:

When DI coverage is provided to you as an employee benefit, you have only two-thirds the coverage you think you have. This is because most employer-provided DI benefits are equal to 60% of your pay. Ordinarily, insurance proceeds are tax-free, but when DI premiums are paid for by your employer, the benefit becomes taxable.

So even though your group policy still pays you only 60% of your pay, this amount is taxable income. You'll lose one-third to taxes, leaving you with only 40% of your pay.

Can you live today on 40% of your current pay?

If not, your employer-provided DI coverage is insufficient for your needs. You need to buy a supplemental DI policy to replace what you'd lose to taxes. You'll discover that this might not be very expensive, because you may not need to buy much coverage, thanks to the amount provided to you by your employer.

**T**alk today with a financial or insurance advisor about obtaining disability income protection.

### How Safe Is Your Occupation?

The more dangerous your job, the more likely it is you'll be hurt. That makes a DI policy more important—and more expensive. Unfortunately, workers in high-risk occupations, such as construction, find that DI coverage either is unusually expensive with benefits payable only for five years or less or is not available at all. In contrast, office workers usually can get coverage at a lower cost with full benefits payable to age 65.

When you submit an application, the insurance company will want to know about your specific job duties, not just your occupation. For example, nurses who work in an administrative capacity pay less for DI coverage than nurses who work in emergency rooms.

Insurance companies also want to know about your avocations, because if you scuba-dive, hang glide, ride motorcycles, or pilot small aircraft you are more likely to become disabled. They price your policy accordingly.

### You Can Lower the Cost by Delaying the Benefits

Say you're injured and unable to work. If you want your insurance company to start sending you checks right away, the cost of your policy will be quite high. But if you're willing to delay for 90 days the start of benefits, you can cut the cost of your policy dramatically.

That's because insurance companies know that most disabilities don't last more than 90 days. If they don't have to pay claims until later, they might not have to pay at all—and that keeps the cost of your policy down.

But if you're out of work for those three months, how will you pay your bills until the insurance kicks in? That's what cash reserves are for—go reread Chapter 2!

## Make Sure Your Benefits Grow with Your Income

All DI policies are based on your income at the time you apply for coverage. Since your income will grow over time, you need a policy whose benefits will grow with increases in your income. Otherwise, the policy that you bought when your income was $30,000 won't be much help if you're disabled when your income is $80,000.

## Make Sure Your Income Grows with Inflation

On a related note, make sure that, once you are disabled, your benefits grow with inflation. After all, if you're permanently disabled, you could be getting checks for decades, and the income you get in the 2000s might not be worth much in the 2020s.

Make sure your policy guarantees automatic increases in your benefits each year or, failing that, offers you the option to increase your coverage with increases in the Consumer Price Index.

## Ask for Benefits to Be Paid for as Long as You Planned to Work

Lots of policies pay benefits for only five years. That's a problem if you're disabled at age 52. Therefore, get a policy that pays benefits to age 65.

As I mentioned earlier, this is not always possible for workers in high-risk occupations or people with preexisting medical conditions. Whatever your situation, seek the longest benefit period you can find.

### Never Ask for Your Money Back

Even people who buy DI policies remain convinced that they'll never become disabled, just as those who buy fire insurance "know" that their house will never burn to the ground.

Since you're buying something you know you won't need, why not insert a clause that enables you to get your money back if you never file a claim?

This option is available. It's called the "Return of Premium Rider" and entitles you to a future refund of the premiums you've paid (usually 50%) if you do not suffer a disability.

It's a dumb option. You buy the policy in case you become disabled, but you buy the rider in case you don't? It doesn't make sense! (You don't do this with your homeowner's or auto policies, do you?)

It makes even less sense when you realize the cost. The rider costs 20% to 40% of your premium, and all it gives you is the possibility of getting back 50% of your money.

When you buy a DI policy, don't ask for your money back. Instead, just hope you never need to file a claim, but rest easy knowing that if you need to, you can.

## Business Owners Should Never Deduct Premiums as a Business Expense

If you're a business owner, you can deduct the cost of your DI policy as a normal business expense. Doing so will give you a tax deduction.

Don't do it.

When an insurance company pays you a claim, that money is tax-free. But if you receive benefits from a policy whose premiums had been treated as a business expense, those benefits are considered taxable income.

Therefore, pay for your DI policy out of your own pocket, not out of your business account. If you don't take the small tax deduction, any disability income payments you later receive will be tax-free.

## LONG-TERM CARE INSURANCE: CAN LIVING A LONG AND HEALTHY LIFE BE A PROBLEM?

Talk about frying pans and fires.

As we've seen—as events of September 11 showed us—you need life insurance to protect your family from the risk that you may die, and you need disability income insurance to protect yourself and your family from the risk that you may become disabled.

And if neither occurs?

Well, then, that means you will live to enjoy your elder years. And there's a good chance you'll do that. Let me recount some statistics I offer in *The Truth About Money:*

- Today, life expectancy at birth is 76. In contrast, life expectancy in ancient Greece was 20. Thousands of years later, around the time of the American Revolution, life expectancy was 23—half of all American colonists were under 16. In 1900, most Americans died by the age of 47.
- Today, 62.7% of all Americans reach age 65. In 1870, only 2.5% did.
- The fastest-growing age group in our country are people over 85.
- If you and your spouse both reach age 65, one of you can be expected to reach age 90.

If death and disability are the frying pans, then old age is the fire.

As you get older, health and medical problems increase. Like I had to tell you that.

But at extreme levels, these aches and pains begin to interfere with the "Activities of Daily Living," a term the health care industry uses to refer to eating, bathing, dressing, toileting, transferring (walking, or getting from bed to chair), and maintaining continence. Because many older Americans incur problems with their ADLs:

- Two out of five people age 65 or older will need long-term care (LTC). More than half of women and about one-third of men will end up in a nursing home.
- Half of those who enter a nursing home will stay six months or less. The other half will stay an average of two-and-a-half years.
- The average cost of a nursing home is $45,000 per year. Half of all older Americans who live alone will spend themselves into poverty after only 13 weeks in a nursing home, while more than half of couples will go broke within six months.

Because so many people face financial ruin due to long-term care costs, I've written extensively about it. In my next book, *Discover the Wealth within You,* due out in April 2002, I delve deeply into the costs of and solutions for long-term care, because 72% of all Americans have already faced these costs or eventually will.

While you're conversant with life insurance and probably already own some, and are somewhat familiar with disability income insurance, it's unlikely that you've ever considered—or even heard of—long-term care insurance.

Indeed, according to one industry study, 50% of consumers have given little or no thought to LTC, and 40% said they'd never even heard of it. These are scary statistics, because long-term care costs have great potential to financially destroy you and your family. That's why I write so much about LTC costs.

Ultimately, I consider LTC costs to be an insurance issue, because insurance is the best way to protect yourself and your family from these exorbitant expenses. But many people dismiss the notion of buying yet another insurance policy. Instead, they assume one of four things:

1. They assume they won't need long-term care.
2. They assume that a member of their family will care for them (usually a spouse or daughter).

3. They assume that the government or their health insurance will pay for their care.
4. They assume they'll have the money to pay for their own care.

We've already dispelled the first myth. Let's consider the other three assumptions.

## Think a Member of Your Family Will Provide Your Care?

Even if you do have a spouse, child, or other relative who is willing and able to care for you, letting this person do so severely damages his or her life and personal finances. Studies show that family caregivers lose $659,139 in lost lifetime wages, pension benefits, and Social Security earnings, usually because they are forced to quit their jobs, retire early, take unpaid leave, convert work to a part-time schedule, use up accrued vacation and sick leave, leave work during the day, arrive late or leave early, pass up a promotion, and/or refuse a job transfer.

Worst of all, 40% of care-giving spouses suffer from depression, and, compared to others their age, those who begin to provide care for their husband or wife are 63% more likely to die within four years.

Are you *sure* you want your spouse or children to be your caregiver?

## Think the Government or Your Health Insurance Will Pay for Your Care?

Surveys show that 34% of Americans think their health insurance will pay for LTC expenses. Another 30% think Medicare will cover the costs, and 14% think Social Security will pay.

All of them are wrong.

Health insurance does not pay for LTC; nor does Social Security or Medicare. What does pay is *Medicaid*, the federal health insurance plan for the poor. Which proves my point: The only way to get government assistance for long-term care is to first become impoverished.

## Think You'll Have the Money to Pay for Your Own Care?

Nationally, the average cost of long-term care is $45,000 per year. That's $3,750 per month.

Say your spouse requires long-term care at that cost. Go to your checkbook right now and write a check for three thousand seven hundred fifty dollars. Can you do it? Good.

Now do it again.

And again.

And again.

And again.

And again.

And again.

And again.

And again.

And again.

And again.

You've just paid for care for 12 months. How many *more* months will you be able to write that check before exhausting your savings? Remember, you have to also pay all of your other household expenses at the same time.

This is why long-term care costs push many people into poverty.

## Should You Pay for the Cost of Care Yourself If You Can Afford It?

Many of those who acknowledge that long-term care costs are in their future intend to pay for the care out of their own pocket. How? They'll just start saving today for the expense.

For most people, that plan won't work.

LTC costs for a 45-year-old are projected to be more than $1.2 million. To save enough to pay that bill, you'd have to save $4,732 per year—on top of other savings! In contrast, that 45-year-old could buy an LTC insurance policy that would cost only $734 per year. Clearly, LTC insurance is much more cost-effective.

Even if you have sufficient assets or income to cover the costs, using your own resources will reduce the money you leave to your spouse, children, community, and other heirs. Are you sure you want to pay for your LTC costs yourself?

---

**That's why, for most people, the best solution is to own LTC insurance. Add it to your auto, homeowner's, life, and DI policies. If you're 50 or older, you need to get this protection now, because the younger you are when you buy it, the more likely you'll medically qualify for a policy and the less expensive it will be.**

---

For example, people in their late 40s will pay about $700 per year. More than 80% of all Americans in this age group can afford this expense, something we can't say for 75-year-olds. Those who wait until that age to pay for a policy will pay more than $5,000 per year—if they can qualify. And only 9% of those over 75 can afford it.

## Seek the Help of an Advisor When Buying Long-Term Care Insurance

Long-term care policies are as complex as disability income policies. Many of the same issues apply: Do you meet the qualifications for receiving benefits, as stipulated in the contract? Who decides? Which expenses are eligible? Will these costs be paid directly by the carrier, or must you pay the expense first and be reimbursed later, after submitting a claim form?

**T**o make sure you're getting the best policy for the best price, rely on the guidance of a financial advisor.

For more on the topic of LTC, including other strategies for paying for it and the features to look for in long-term care insurance policies, see Chapter 72 of *The Truth About Money* and watch for the release of my new book, *Discover the Wealth Within You*.

## AUTO INSURANCE: LET'S LOOK AT THE DECLARATION PAGE

If you own a car, you have auto insurance. That means you get a thick envelope periodically from your automobile insurance carrier. Most important in that packet is the declaration page, which identifies the amount of coverage you have and how much you pay for it. Let's review some of the basic information featured on that page:

1. THE INSURED. This is the person named on the policy. Coverage is usually extended to persons related to the insured who are members of the insured's household.

   In most states if a teenage driver not listed as one of the insureds has an accident, the insurance company is likely to:
   a. rebill the insured for the extra costs of the teenage driver for the period the teenager has held a driver's license,
   b. settle the claim, then
   c. cancel the policy.

2. THE DRIVER'S LICENSE NUMBER OF EACH DRIVER. When you're seeking rate quotes, expect each auto insurance company to investigate the driving record of each driver before giving you a quote.

3. LIABILITY COVERAGE. This is the maximum amount that the policy will pay to cover medical bills for people (other than your immediate family) you hurt with your vehicle. Liability coverage is quoted as:
   a. the maximum amount payable to any one person,
   b. the maximum amount payable for all medical claims, and
   c. the maximum amount payable for claims of property damage.

---

Each state requires that drivers maintain certain minimum amounts of liability coverage. Ignore these minimums and instead carry the *maximum* that your state permits.

---

4. COLLISION. Collision covers damage to the car when it is in operation.
5. COMPREHENSIVE (ALSO KNOWN AS OTHER THAN COLLISION). Comprehensive covers damage to the vehicle when the car is not in operation. Typical causes are vandalism, theft, and really bad weather.
6. MEDICAL. Your auto policy's medical coverage covers only those expenses associated with auto accidents; the amount of coverage in most auto policies is less than $10,000. Therefore, if you have an excellent health insurance policy, this coverage is unnecessary. By dropping this feature, you can lower the cost of the policy or use the savings to boost other, more important aspects of coverage.
7. PERSONAL INJURY PROTECTION. PIP includes disability and medical benefits, so if you have separate disability and medical insurance, drop PIP (although some states require you to maintain it).
8. UNINSURED MOTORIST. This coverage pays your medical bills if an uninsured motorist injures you or a passenger in your car. It will also pay for damage to your vehicle.

Although your health insurance will pay your medical bills and your collision coverage will pay for damages if an uninsured motorist hits you, which duplicates this feature, uninsured motorist coverage also compensates you for "pain and suffering," which the others do not.

Note that your auto insurance protects you and your car in the United States and Canada, not Mexico.

## Tips to Reduce the Cost of Your Auto Insurance

Insurance companies and their agents get nervous when drivers drop any portion of their coverage, not just because they lose some of their commissions, but because they fear you might later sue them if you have a claim that is not covered.

Therefore, before you drop any coverage, explain to your agent what you plan to do and why. See if the agent can give a valid reason why you shouldn't drop it. Consider his or her input before you make a decision.

Here are strategies to lower your auto insurance premiums:

- If your car is worth less than $3,000 and paid for, consider dropping both the collision and comprehensive coverages. If your car is worth only a couple thousand dollars, is it worth paying $100 or more per year to protect against the chance your car might be totaled in an accident?
- Increase your policy's deductibles. By paying the first $500 or $1,000 of any loss, instead of just $100 or $250, you can cut your premiums by 10% to 20% per year.
- When shopping for your next car, consider the costs of insuring it. Sports cars and convertibles are more expensive to insure than other cars. Cars equipped with antilock brakes, air bags, antitheft devices, and automatic seat belts cost less to insure, as do cars that are less expensive to repair. The next time you buy a car, check first with your auto

insurance agent to see which of the cars you're considering are the cheapest to insure.

- Drive safely. Each traffic ticket or accident will increase your premiums for five years.
- See if your insurance company will offer you a discount for completing a defensive driving class. If so, take the class.
- The amount you pay for insurance is directly related to the number of miles you drive each year. Insurers note the distance between your home and office. To lower your rate, live close to work or, better yet, do not drive to work.
- If you and your family insure more than one car, use one insurance company to obtain a multicar discount. If you use one of your cars infrequently, seek lower rates on that vehicle.
- You may qualify for further discounts if you insure your cars with the same company that insures your house.
- Pay for your policy with one check per year, instead of paying in monthly, quarterly, or semiannual installments. Paying in full at one time can save you substantial amounts of money.
- As with any major purchase, comparison shop to save money. Rates for identical coverage can vary by more than 300%. But also investigate each insurer's reputation; some that charge low rates insure only drivers with impeccable driving records; any accident or ticket could result in cancellation of your coverage.
- You might receive a more competitive quote from a local agent by visiting his or her office instead of doing business via telephone or the Internet. Before the appointment, wash the car and dress like you're being interviewed—because you are. Many agents and companies evaluate the perceived maturity of the driver as they determine what rates to offer.
- Get quotes from at least three different companies. Companies use dozens of variables to calculate your rate. Some will even reduce your rate if you don't smoke or drink.

■ Your cost is partly determined by where you garage your car. If you change where your car is kept, tell your insurance company. It may lower your rate (or raise it!). More important, failure to do so could result in cancellation of your policy.

## HOMEOWNER'S INSURANCE: YOUR HUMBLE ABODE

If you own your home (with or without a mortgage), homeowner's insurance protects the value of the house as well as its contents. If you rent your home, renter's insurance covers only the contents. Both types offer medical protection and liability coverage.

### Are You Prepared to Be Homeless?

**I**f you don't have homeowner's or renter's coverage, you could become homeless and possessionless at any time. Buy this insurance immediately. It's remarkably inexpensive.

Whether you rent or own, your policy covers personal items that are lost, destroyed, or stolen, whether the items are stolen from your home or while the items are with you while you are away (including personal items stolen from your car).

There are two types of property:

REAL PROPERTY: This type of property is attached to the earth or to the house. For example, not only is your house real property, but so is the chandelier that hangs from the ceiling.

PERSONAL PROPERTY: A lamp merely plugged into the wall is considered personal property. Make sure your personal items—including clothing, furniture, televisions, and computers—are insured for their "replacement cost," not their "actual cash value." If your items are lost, destroyed, or stolen, you want the insurance company to give you enough money to buy replacements, not merely reimburse you for the items' current (used) values.

## Be Able to Prove What You Owned

The insurance company won't pay you for a missing personal item unless you can prove that you owned it. Here's how to do it:

1. Whenever you buy an item of insurable value, record its serial number on the receipt and store the receipt in a safe place.
2. Photograph or videotape expensive items. When imaging your property, be sure the frame includes a reference point for sizing. For example, have someone stand next to a table to provide some indication of its size. When you photograph a smaller item, such as jewelry, place a ruler alongside it.
3. Duplicate the video or photos. Keep the duplicate at a different location, since if the house burns down, the video or photos will be destroyed along with everything else! Update the video and photos as needed.
4. Engrave your driver's license number on expensive items. Include your state's initials.
5. Include your clothing in the above. Although losing one shirt or blouse might not be worth filing a claim, having to replace your entire wardrobe because of fire, theft, or water damage could cost thousands of dollars.

## Are Your Fine Arts Covered?

Most policies do not cover paintings, rare coins and stamps, jewelry, or collections. You'll need to buy a rider for these items, describing each in detail. A professional appraisal for each item is usually required; keep the appraisal with the rest of your receipts. Insurance companies often also demand that you install a burglar alarm before they agree to insure valuable personal items.

## The Liability Protection Feature

This feature protects you and your property from the claims of others—such as the postal carrier your dog bit, the child who was hurt playing in your pool, the neighbor who slipped on your icy sidewalk, or the guest who tripped down your stairs. Standard policies pay only $25,000—that's far too little.

> **M**ake sure your policy provides liability coverage of at least five times your annual household income or twice your family's net worth, whichever is greater. The cost is quite affordable.

## The Medical Protection Feature

This protects your visitors, not immediate family members who live with you, and pays even if the guest is at fault. There is no deductible. If the injury is your fault, your liability feature will take over after your medical coverage has been exhausted.

## The Real Property Protection Feature

> **I**f you're a homeowner, check to make sure that your home is insured for its replacement cost. And verify that the policy reflects your home's current value.

Every house can be valued in many ways. Consider the following figures. They all refer to the same house:

- Purchase price (what you paid to buy it): $200,000
- Current mortgage balance (what you owe the lender): $130,000
- Appraised value (what it's supposedly worth): $210,000
- Assessed value (for calculating property taxes): $190,000
- Current market value (what people should pay to buy it): $300,000
- Equity value (its liquidation value to you): $170,000
- Replacement cost (your cost to replace it): $250,000

This house should be insured for $250,000. Why is the replacement cost less than the current market value? Because the CMV includes the cost of the land—and that's something you probably won't have to replace (more on that later).

You should have your house appraised every five to seven years to verify that you still have proper insurance amounts on it. You also should review your coverage whenever you remodel or expand the home.

## Are You Likely to Experience a Natural Disaster?

Most people need to insure only the house, not the land it sits on. But in many parts of the country, homeowners also must protect against losing the land as a result of earthquakes or floods.

EARTHQUAKES: Earthquake coverage in areas that require it is expensive. The deductible is high—often $10,000 or more. The rider is added to the homeowner's policy, although Californians must purchase a separate policy. In most cases, earthquake coverage increases the cost of insurance by 50% or more.

FLOODS: Standard homeowner policies do not cover flood damage. If you live in a flood plain, call the National Flood Insurance

Program at 800-638-6620. The policy is not effective until 31 days after you buy it.

---

**D**espite these extra costs, you'd be foolish to own homes in such areas without these protections. If you don't already have coverage, get it today.

---

## Five Ways to Reduce the Cost of Your Homeowner's Insurance

Keep these points in mind about your policy:

- Do not file small claims. Reserve your claims for major losses. After two or three claims of any size many insurance companies either increase the premium or cancel the policy.
- Increase your deductible to lower your premium. Changing it from $100 to $1,000 can save you 20% to 35% per year. If you ever have a claim, use your cash reserves to cover the deductible or any small losses.
- If you are buying a home, see if buying a new one instead of a resale will get you a discount on your policy. Homes built in the last 10 years may also qualify for a discount. Because wood homes are more susceptible to fire than brick homes, they cost about 15% more to insure.
- The more safety features, the lower the premium. To cut your premium by up to 20%, add the following safety features:
  - Dead bolt locks
  - Burglar alarms
  - Smoke detectors
  - Fire extinguishers

- Ask for discounts. Insurers often offer lower rates if:
  - No one in the household smokes.
  - You have been with the same company for five years or more.

If you have questions about your policy that your agent or insurance company cannot answer to your satisfaction, call the Insurance Information Institute's hot line at 800-942-4242, or call your state's Department of Insurance.

## PROTECTING YOUR FAMILY FROM LAWSUITS

It's sad, but we can expect lawyers to file lawsuits as a result of events that took place on September 11. When something bad happens, lawsuits are often the result.

It reminds us of our need to protect ourselves and our family against legal liabilities. You are liable to be sued if a guest in your home falls down your stairs or if you are involved in an auto accident. You could be sued for millions, and juries are unpredictable; you never know the amount they might award.

### The Three Types of Liability

Liability risks often are not understood. Let's review three liability exposures you face:

1. PERSONAL. You or a member of your household could be judged liable for harming someone.
2. PROPERTY. You or a member of your household could be judged liable for damaging someone's property.
3. PROFESSIONAL. If you harm someone or his or her property while you're carrying out the duties of your occupation, both you and your company are at risk of liability.

## The Three Types of Costs You Could Incur

If you are found liable, you could face costs in three categories:

PROPERTY DAMAGES: If you, your child, or your property (such as your car) damage someone else's property, you could be required to pay for the costs of repairing or replacing the other party's property.

MEDICAL EXPENSES: You could be responsible for the costs incurred by those whom you or your family member have injured.

PAIN AND SUFFERING: These costs are both difficult to quantify and often higher than the actual property and medical costs. Awards for pain and suffering are intended to punish you.

## BUY AN UMBRELLA BEFORE IT RAINS: UMBRELLA LIABILITY COVERAGE

Most auto and homeowner's policies limit liability coverage to $500,000 or less. Yet, as I mentioned, liability from lawsuits represent your largest financial risk. This means that if all you own are auto and homeowner's policies, you do not have enough protection from potential lawsuits.

As the name implies, umbrella liability policies help protect you for nearly anything that might go wrong. These policies typically cost under $250 per year for $1 million in protection. Because they're so inexpensive, many carriers will sell you a policy only if you buy your homeowner's and auto coverage from them as well.

**B**uy an umbrella liability insurance policy today.

## CHAPTER 6

# Create or Update Your Estate Plan

THE MORE THAN SIX THOUSAND people who perished in the hijackings and attacks on the World Trade Center and Pentagon on September 11 left behind many more thousands of family members, who in addition to bearing the human loss must soon turn their attention to legal matters. The bank, brokerage, and real estate holdings, as well as personal possessions, of the deceased will have to be transferred to the survivors.

It's likely that most of the people who were killed in the attack had bank accounts.

They probably also had IRA accounts and owned mutual funds and other investments, in addition to annuities and insurance policies.

They may have had business interests.

They likely participated in a retirement plan at work and owned a car, a house, and personal belongings.

Some of these personal items, such as watches and jewelry, collections, audio and video equipment, furniture, and artwork, have significant financial value.

Other personal possessions are of little economic worth but huge sentimental value—family heirlooms, mementos, photos, and personal records.

All of these items must be tabulated for legal and tax purposes and distributed to the heirs.

Who, exactly, are the heirs?

## WHO ARE YOUR HEIRS?

Few people die leaving no one behind. Commonly, mourners include a husband or wife, children, parents, brothers and sisters, aunts and uncles, grandparents, nieces and nephews, godchildren, close friends or partners (business or personal), colleagues, neighbors, and mentors. And increasingly in today's society, there also are ex-spouses, stepchildren, and lots and lots of in-laws, both current and ex.

Who, exactly, gets what?

If you haven't stated—in writing—who you want to receive your property in the event of your death, you have guaranteed that your surviving spouse and children will suffer, because you have imposed on them unnecessary legal costs and taxes and substantial wastes of time—all on top of the emotional trauma that your death itself will inflict on them.

Fortunately, most of these potential problems are completely and easily avoidable. All you have to do are two simple things:

1. **Decide who gets what.**
2. **Call a lawyer.**

An estate attorney, a lawyer who practices in the field of wills and trusts, will do the rest for you. It will cost as little as $150; even full-blown estate plans for multimillionaires don't cost more than

$5,000. (People who need to spend that much for comprehensive estate planning can easily afford it; if you can't afford it, that means you don't need it, so don't fret over it.)

If you don't have a lawyer, ask your financial planner or tax preparer for a referral, or get the name of a good attorney from friends, family, or your local bar association.

People sometimes ask me when they ought to get a will. My answer is simple: Get one before you die—meaning make your list and call a lawyer today.

In the rest of this chapter, I'll explain how everything works. But please don't let yourself get caught up in the details. Just focus on what you own and who you want to receive it. Implementing your wishes is your lawyer's job.

## PUT YOUR WISHES IN WRITING

You tell the world who gets what by writing a document called a "will." In this document, which your lawyer will write for you (saying in legalese what you want it to say), you leave instructions for the disposition of your assets. Typically, your will tells your survivors:

- Which debts to eliminate (such as auto loans) and which to retain (such as mortgages);
- Which assets to sell (such as real estate or businesses) and which to keep (such as heirlooms);
- Who is to receive which assets (financial and sentimental);
- When to distribute those assets (immediately, at some future time, or when certain conditions are satisfied);
- Who is to take legal responsibility for any children under the age of 18;
- Who is to ensure that your instructions are implemented (this person is called your "executor" or "personal representative").

If, by the time you die, you have failed to write a will, or one that will be deemed valid by the state in which you live, you will be considered to have died "intestate." Your property will be distributed in accordance with state law rather than your desires. This means your money could go to children from a prior marriage rather than to your current spouse. It could mean, depending on where you live, that your parents or in-laws get your money instead of the people you wish to have it.

In addition, if you don't leave a valid will, a judge will decide who will raise your minor-age children. To prevent this, you must name a guardian in your will. To learn how to choose the best person for the job, see Chapter 77 of *The Truth About Money*. There I also explain that minors are not permitted to own assets and therefore you need to place into trust the money you plan to leave your minor children.

## NO SPOUSE, NO KIDS, NO FAMILY, NO FRIENDS?

Most people think that only those with a spouse and children need a will.

Wrong.

Everyone needs a will. Or rather, everyone who has stuff needs a will. If you own no property and have no assets, then, okay, maybe it's not all that important.

But even if you have no spouse, no kids, no family, and no friends, if you have stuff, you still need to write a will. Why?

Because you have a community who needs you.

Please tell us which charitable or community organization is to receive your worldly possessions. A lot of people are depending on you—even if you don't know their names.

# ESTATE LAWS FAVOR MARRIED COUPLES

When a married person dies, his or her surviving spouse enjoys many protections under the law. For example, surviving spouses are entitled by law to receive their deceased spouse's retirement assets, even if the deceased didn't leave such instructions—or named someone else!

People who are close to you but aren't married to you have no such protection. This includes not only children but a lover you intend to marry. If your partner is not your spouse, your partner enjoys no legal protections, even if the wedding day has been set.

If you die unmarried and without a will, your parents, and not your betrothed, could easily receive your assets.

Even single people need a will.

# MARRIED PEOPLE SHOULD AVOID THE "SIMPLE WILL"

In a "simple will," you leave everything to your spouse or to your children if your spouse dies sooner than you. This is what most married people do, but it's often a bad strategy.

Consider this chronology of events:

1. You have a spouse and children.
2. You die, leaving everything to your spouse.
3. Your spouse remarries someone who has children from a prior marriage.
4. Your spouse then dies, leaving everything to the new spouse.
5. The new spouse dies, leaving everything to his or her kids.
6. Your kids get nothing.

Yuk.

This is the type of problem that simple wills can create. It's better to leave your money to a trust, not to your spouse.

Consider *this* chronology of events:

1. You have a spouse and children.
2. You die, leaving everything to a trust for the benefit of your spouse. Your spouse receives income and principal from the trust for the remainder of his or her lifetime.
3. Your spouse remarries someone who has children from a prior marriage.
4. Your spouse then dies.
5. Since your spouse didn't own the money—it's still in the trust—your spouse can't bequeath that money to his or her new spouse. Instead, the trust's assets will benefit your children.

Since you're the one creating the trust, you can impose whatever rules you want for the management and distribution of its assets and income.

## WHAT IF YOUR HEIRS CAN'T HANDLE MONEY?

Do you really want to leave all your money to your 18-year-old? What about relatives who have drug or alcohol problems, who gamble, who can't hold a job, or who are abusive?

What about relatives who never seem to have any money, who are always bouncing checks, who live paycheck to paycheck, who owe you lots of money, and who are constantly borrowing more from you and others?

Do you really want to leave your money to people like this? Of course you do, because you love them. So it might be better to leave your money to a trust. You can have the trust distribute assets or income to these heirs slowly or under certain conditions.

For example, you can delay distributions until the heirs reach certain ages (in the hope they'll be more mature by then), or you can distribute the money over time, like an allowance.

You can distribute interest only, keeping the principal in the trust. This will protect the heirs from blowing all the cash and ending up in poverty.

You can require that the money be used only to pay for college, obtain medical care, or buy a home.

It's your money and your trust, so lay down any rules you want.

## TITLE YOUR ASSETS CAREFULLY

As important as it is that you write a will, please realize that your will does not determine the fate of much of your assets.

That's because assets pass to heirs in two ways, not just one. The first, as we've discussed, is via the will. But for the following assets we follow something called Operation of Law, and the will is ignored:

- IRA accounts,
- retirement accounts,
- annuities,
- life insurance policies,
- trusts.

When you obtain any of these assets, you are asked to name the beneficiary for it. Whoever you write down on the form will receive that asset upon your death. (For most employer-provided retirement plans, married people must name their spouse as the primary beneficiary; naming anyone else requires the spouse's written consent.)

Operation of Law also applies for savings or investment accounts you own with another person. There are three types of "joint accounts":

- JOINT TENANCY WITH RIGHTS OF SURVIVORSHIP. The JTWROS is the most common type of joint account. Each person is deemed to own half the property, although transactions affecting the entire account may be executed by either (unless the pair agree to require two signatures). When one dies, the other inherits the account.

- ■ TENANTS BY THE ENTIRETY. This can be used only by married couples, and each spouse is deemed to own 100% of the asset. This offers greater protection against creditors. With a JTWROS account, if you are sued, your half of the account can be claimed by your creditor, but with a TbyE account, since your spouse is deemed to own 100% of the account, creditors can't reach it so easily. In a TbyE, as with a JTWROS, when one spouse dies, the other inherits the account.

- ■ TENANTS IN COMMON. This may be used by nonspouses, and there can be an unlimited number of co-owners (or "tenants") to the account. Each tenant owns a share of the asset, but when any tenant dies, his or her share is not inherited by the remaining tenants; instead, it is conveyed to the deceased's heirs in accordance with his or her will. This means that when one of the owners dies, the surviving tenants will find themselves with a new co-owner, whether they like it or not.

Any asset that (a) does not feature a named beneficiary or (b) is not jointly held will be distributed to heirs via the will.

If you have a bank account in your name only, your will controls its distribution. But before the will's instructions can be followed, the will must be deemed valid by the probate court—a process that involves time, money, and public scrutiny. But if you add a second person's name to the bank account, Operation of Law takes over. This enables the asset to be passed to heirs quickly, quietly, and inexpensively.

Sometimes, you can decide which way to go. For example, you can leave the truck titled in your name only (forcing the truck to go to your brother via probate) or you can add your brother's name to the title (enabling him to inherit the truck immediately upon your death).

In many cases, you don't have a choice. After all, your big-screen TV doesn't have a "title." Neither does your collection of Elvis Presley records. These assets must go through probate. (Are you starting to see why a will is so important?)

Many people prefer to avoid probate wherever possible, and that makes sense. Unfortunately, doing it the wrong way could cost thousands.

## AVOIDING PROBATE

### The Wrong Way: Title Everything Jointly with Your Spouse or Child

To avoid probate, you could just title all your assets jointly with your spouse (provided you have a spouse). This works fine, but it puts you back into the trap of the simple will that I described earlier. It also creates another potential problem: If you die in 2002 or later with more than $1 million in assets, holding everything jointly with your spouse can cause your kids to lose hundreds of thousands of dollars to estate taxes.

This problem is particularly acute for people who add their child's name to their property. When you do that, your *heir* becomes your *co-owner*. The result?

- **YOU TRIGGER CAPITAL GAINS TAXES.** Instead of inheriting the asset free of capital gains tax, as an heir would do, the co-owner must now pay taxes on any capital gains when he or she sells the property. Thus, a tax is due unnecessarily.
- **YOU WASTE YOUR TIME.** If the child dies first, you'll wind up owning the asset by yourself all over again—and again

without an heir. And if you can't prove that you added the child's name to the account strictly for the convenience of inheritance, the IRS will assume that the child owned 50% of the asset, potentially creating a tax liability where none should have existed.

- **YOU GET ROBBED.** Naming your child as a co-owner gives the child legal access to the asset. Might he steal it? If it's a bank account, might she "borrow" some of it without notifying you?

- **YOU GET SUED.** You could lose some or all of your asset if your child is sued. As I explained earlier, your son's car accident could cost you your asset—simply because you placed his name on your bank account.

- **YOU DISINHERIT OTHER CHILDREN.** When people place one child's name on their bank account, deed to the house, or brokerage account, they usually do so because that one child helps a lot with daily affairs. What they don't realize is that the will—which states that all the kids are to be equal heirs—is then nullified. That one child gets all the assets, and the other children have little or no legal recourse. (If the child tries to fulfill the parent's intent by giving some of the money to his or her siblings, doing so can result in gift taxes!)

- **YOU HURT THE CHILD'S FINANCIAL STANDING.** The IRS has ruled against people who claimed deductions involving property titled with parents. You also can reduce a child's ability to qualify for financial aid, because of his or her joint ownership of your asset.

Avoiding probate is a sound goal. Just don't try to do it by adding your children's names to your accounts. Instead, let's avoid probate the right way.

## The Right Way: The Revocable Living Trust

All you need to do is establish a Revocable Living Trust and title all of your assets into it. It's that simple.

Thus, you won't have a bank account anymore. Instead, you'll have a trust that has a bank account. It sounds complicated, but it isn't. The only real difference is that your checks will have the word "trustee" after your name. You'll still enjoy full ownership and control over your assets (along with the same tax liabilities).

The point is that revocable trusts avoid probate. You get to name beneficiaries, distribute your assets as you wish, keep your decisions private, and, perhaps best of all, make it harder for disgruntled heirs to complain. Your trust can also help you manage your assets during your lifetime if you become incompetent.

Paying a lawyer to draft a trust document isn't enough when establishing a Revocable Living Trust. After you sign the papers, it's critical that you retitle your assets into the name of the trust. It's easy to do—just contact your bank or financial advisor. Remember, a trust is like a vault: It's of no value unless its holds assets.

## The Lazy Way to Avoid Probate

Another, easier, way to avoid probate without turning heirs into owners is to take advantage of Transfer on Death and Payable on Death registrations.

TOD registration is used for securities; POD titling is used for bank accounts. Both enable you to name heirs directly on the accounts, avoiding both the will and probate.

If an asset is registered as "John Jones TOD Jeffrey Jones, Freda Jones, and Alice Jones," Jeffrey, Freda, and Alice will inherit it upon John's death. The asset avoids probate as well the other problems I described earlier.

TOD and POD registrations do not solve estate planning problems as comprehensively as Revocable Living Trusts, but setting up TOD and POD accounts is quick, easy, and free.

## LIVING WILLS

If you are in a coma (or "persistent vegetative state"), do you want your life extended through artificial means, or would you prefer to be allowed to die naturally, with support provided only for your comfort and alleviation of pain?

Your answer belongs in a document called a Living Will. In it, you state your preferences regarding medical treatment in the event of terminal illness or injury.

---

**W**hen you meet with your attorney, ask for a Living Will.

---

## DURABLE POWERS OF ATTORNEY FOR HEALTH CARE

Having a Living Will is fine, but when the time comes, you'll be in no condition to demand that its instructions are followed. That's why you need a second document, a Durable Power of Attorney for Health Care.

By signing this document, you grant another person (usually a spouse or other family member) the legal right to make medical decisions for you. They'll decide what kind of medical treatment you should receive, such as surgery, and if necessary they'll carry out your wishes as you stated them in your Living Will.

---

**M**any states have combined the Living Will and the Durable Power of Attorney for Health Care into one document called a Medical Directive. Be certain you obtain it, and verify that the person you designate as your "attorney in fact" is willing to follow your instructions.

---

## DURABLE GENERAL POWER OF ATTORNEY

While you're in the hospital, someone needs to tend to your mail, pay your bills, and feed the cat. But who will have access to your home and bank accounts?

A Durable General Power of Attorney allows another person (again, usually a spouse) to sign legal documents for you and handle financial affairs for you. The person you name can use your checkbook to pay bills, sell securities to obtain cash for medical expenses, file your income tax return, and renew leases.

Make sure this power is *durable,* for ordinary powers become void when you are incapacitated.

You are granting the person you name in this document unlimited access and control of all your assets, so choose someone you trust without reservation.

---

**A**fter granting someone your Durable General Power of Attorney, take a copy of the document to your bank and financial advisor to see if they'll accept it. Often, financial institutions require that their own forms be used, and many reject powers of attorney that are as little as six months old. Make sure your document will do what you want it to do.

---

## DEATH AND TAXES

I have discussed the administrative issues pertaining to estate planning, to help you make sure that your assets will go to the people you want them to go to. Another consideration is estate taxes.

You and your heirs will not incur any estate taxes if your assets are worth less than $675,000—$1 million beginning January 1 2002—so most Americans don't have to worry about it.

There also are no capital gains taxes to worry about, because all capital gains produced during your lifetime pass to heirs tax-free upon your death. (This will change in 2010, but it's not worth worrying about today.)

Likewise, life insurance proceeds are tax-free (although the amount paid in death benefits counts toward that $675,000 limit, which could result in an estate tax).

Your assets could be subject to income taxes, however. Money that is distributed to heirs from IRAs, company retirement accounts, and annuities are subject to federal income taxes, at rates as high as 39.6%, as well as state income taxes. It is beyond the scope of this book to provide a comprehensive review of the tax avoidance strategies available to those engaging in estate planning, so if your assets are worth more than $675,000, or if you have money in IRAs, retirement plans, or annuities, be sure to talk with your financial advisor or attorney.

You can also consult Parts 9–12 of *The Truth About Money*, but be aware that recent regulatory changes have rendered outdated the section on taxing IRAs.

## THE MOST IMPORTANT ESTATE PLANNING STRATEGY

Talk with your family tonight about your estate plan—and about theirs, too. Never keep your plans a secret.

As I discuss in *Ordinary People, Extraordinary Wealth*, the most financially successful people in the United States do not keep secrets about their wills and trusts from their children or their parents.

Do you know what your parents plan to leave you?

Have you told your kids what you plan to leave them?

**W**ith the events of September 11 painfully fresh in our minds and hearts, now is the time to have these frank, detailed, honest, and open conversations with your family.

My colleagues and I have seen it all.

We've seen brothers argue over the handling of their mother's estate.

We've seen nieces ex-communicate their aunt until she agreed to sign over the deed to a family beach house she had owned jointly with her sister.

We've seen children sue their stepmother, their father's widow.

When a client died of cancer, we saw his three-year-old child lose her inheritance, as his former wife manipulated the money away from her, legally but unethically. This happened because the father had failed to properly sign a document, and his widow—the child's mother—could do nothing to stop it.

We've seen clients fly to their mother's home after getting the news of her death, discovering when they arrived that the house had been ransacked by relatives who lived nearby. Jewelry, photos, and mementos had been removed, and legal battles ensued.

We've seen a brother sue his sister for refusing to sell the beach house they both inherited after their parents died. He needed the money; she enjoyed taking her kids to the ocean. A judge settled the matter, and her kids will never see their uncle again.

We've seen a grandfather set up a trust to benefit the grandson he hadn't seen in the 12 years since his son got divorced. When the boy's mother heard about it, she initially tried to prevent the boy from receiving the money, worried that the grandfather had "ulterior motives."

We've seen parents leave huge amounts of a single stock to their children, who treated it like an heirloom and not a financial asset. The stock market's decline of the past 18 months has caused the kids to lose more than half the value of their inheritance.

We've seen a 23-year-old son inherit $500,000 when his parents, both in their early 50s, died only months apart. Within a year, the money was gone, spent on parties, cars, clothes, and friends.

We've seen parents leave all their money to their kids equally, ignoring the fact that one of their children is a drug addict. Since none of his inheritance is now left, his sisters find themselves financially responsible for him.

We've seen parents disinherit their son, a successful business executive, leaving their money to their other children, who were struggling financially. But they never explained their motives, leaving their son wondering why his parents cut him off. His children, too, don't understand why they didn't get the same inheritance their cousins received. It's left them bitter toward their grandparents and uncomfortable around their cousins, who have bragged about their inheritances.

I've seen parents give money to their grandchildren, only to have their son later lose custody of the children after his divorce. The parents, in effect, have given money—now controlled by their ex-daughter-in-law—to grandchildren they will never see again.

We've seen parents disinherit their son the beach bum, fearing he'd just squander any money they left him. After their death, the son turned to his siblings, demanding that they support him since their parents left him with no share of the inheritance. This turned the siblings into surrogate parents.

All of these stories are true, and in none of them did the deceased intend to create such conflicts within the family. In every case, poor or nonexistent communication and insufficient estate planning were at the root of the problem. Children and relatives did not know the deceased's desires, intentions, motivations, or rationale and were left to guess or, worse, take matters into their own hands. In none of these stories did money produce happiness.

Make sure this doesn't happen to your family. In Chapter 5, I said that the worst thing is dealing with bill collectors while experiencing the grief of losing a loved one. But in fact, the *worst* is when all that is accompanied by destroyed relationships within the family.

It is up to you to make sure this does not occur. You can prevent these problems with proper estate planning and open communication with your spouse, parents, siblings, children, in-laws, and step relations.

Make that first phone call tonight, for as I've said elsewhere, the one asset you must pass on is

**peace.**

## CHAPTER 7

# The Investment Strategy You Need Today

A T THIS TIME THE Dow Jones Industrial Average has fallen 6% since September 11. The S&P 500 has fallen 3%, and the Nasdaq has dropped 7%.

These recent declines have made the past two years even worse than they had already been. Since January 2000, the Dow has dropped 20%; the S&P 500, 27%; and the Nasdaq, 62%.

Let's face it: A lot of people have lost a lot of money in the past two years. And now the news is filled with worries that the aftermath of the attack on America is going to push the United States into a recession. Already, hundreds of thousands of employees in the airline, hotel, restaurant, travel, convention, hospitality, and retail industries have lost their jobs. More layoffs are expected. Will home sales begin to decline? Many think so, which would create a problem for the real estate, mortgage banking, and construction industries. The dominoes could then hit the automotive industry as people stop making major purchases.

It's easy to portray economic malaise from all this. In light of this, what changes do we recommend for our clients' investment portfolios?

None.

To be sure, we are carefully—and repeatedly—reviewing our clients' investments. But, to date, our conclusion has been that no changes are warranted in their portfolios. Of course, we realize that this could change at any time as events unfold. That's why we keep watching the news, studying the markets, evaluating the investments we've recommended, and communicating with our clients. Nonetheless, at this time we see nothing on the horizon to lead us to believe that we need to modify the investments that our clients own; nor do we believe that we'll need to change this outlook (although of course we're constantly retesting that hypothesis).

Because our clients own carefully designed, highly diversified long-term portfolios, they can now sit tight with their money. But this doesn't mean that you should. Quite the contrary. That's because most investors' portfolios aren't like the ones our clients have, and as a result, sitting tight is the last thing most investors—you?—should be doing.

## Have You Gotten Yourself into Another Fine Mess, Ollie?

Sadly (but predictably, if you've been tuning in to my radio and TV shows or reading my newsletter for the past five years), too many consumers have only recently discovered that they are not the investment geniuses they thought they were. Here are just a few of the cocky—and unsustainable—sentiments many people expressed in the late 1990s:

*Who needs insurance? My quadrupling-every-quarter tech stocks will solve all my family's financial needs!*

*Who needs to diversify? The more money you put in other investments, the less you have in Internet stocks! People who diversify are missing out on lost profits.*

*Who needs to own bonds? Government bonds are for old ladies! The real action is in eBay, Cisco, Nortel, Amazon.com, AOL, and dozens more like them.*

*Why leave money in cash? If I need money, I'll just sell a few shares of stock. My online discount broker will send it to me any time I ask, and in the meantime, I can keep all my money fully invested so it'll keep doubling in value.*

*Who needs to hire a financial advisor? I get all the hot stock tips I need from Motley Fool, and it's free!*

You would be amazed how much difficulty we had convincing people in 1998 and 1999 to stay out of technology stocks and avoid all the new dotcom stocks coming onto the market. Consumers kept hearing stories of people who had turned small investments into huge fortunes in remarkably short periods of time, and they wanted to know how to cash in, too.

Today, the people who never bought Internet mutual funds and technology stocks consider themselves fortunate (and, often, vindicated). Although their portfolio didn't double in a year, they have not lost 95% of it, either.

The hapless investors who once thought tech stocks were the key to wealth have learned the error of their ways. They've quit day trading and gotten real jobs again; they're buying mutual funds once more; and even Motley Fool—which has laid off most of its 400 or so staff after reportedly suffering huge financial losses, has fired its chief executive, and has seen one of its three founders quit to become a producer at ESPN (not exactly known for its financial coverage)—has now hooked up with a financial planning firm to provide its online users with advice—for a fee.

So much for the fools of the late 1990s.

## IT'S NO LONGER FUN AND GAMES

Yes, like everyone else who had avoided Nasdaq's losses, we'd been feeling a little smug. Until September 11, that terrible day when all humor and confidence were instantly—albeit temporarily—sapped out of America. Today, like everyone else, we wonder if any of the old rules still apply, and we wonder what's going to come next.

No one can predict the future, of course, and we'd be the last to try. But one thing is certain: The United States of America will emerge from our current troubles far stronger than we are today, and this is the only fact we need to guide us as we develop effective, safe, *and profitable* investment strategies for the future.

So let me show you how to build the type of investment portfolio you should have had in the first place, so you're better able to survive our current economic environment and thrive in the next one.

> **Own a carefully designed, highly diversified long-term portfolio.**

Let's examine this statement piece by piece.

## FIRST, MAKE SURE YOUR PORTFOLIO IS <u>CAREFULLY DESIGNED</u>

Too often, people's portfolios look like their attics: There's a whole bunch of stuff in there—most of it junk—and nobody knows how it got there, what it was for, or why it wasn't thrown out years ago.

Does your portfolio look like an attic, or the lobby of the Waldorf-Astoria?

When we design an investment portfolio for a client, the first thing we do is evaluate his or her need for cash reserves (that's why I delayed discussing investment strategies until now but talked about cash reserves in Chapter 2). Only after we have verified that the client has sufficient cash reserves do we begin to contemplate what his or her investment portfolio should look like.

---

**T**herefore, the first thing you need to do is set aside sufficient cash reserves.

---

People often call us because they are interested in opening a mutual fund account. Sometimes, our initial phone conversation reveals that they owe thousands of dollars to credit cards and all they've got is a few hundred dollars in a bank account. Sorry, we tell them, you need to pay off the debt first, accumulate several thousand dollars in cash reserves, and *then* call us to open a mutual fund account. I suspect that, after we hang up the phone, many of them call another firm to get what they want.

Once, while appearing on a popular television show, I made the mistake of saying that you can open a mutual account with as little as $100 (actually, many funds let you open an account with just $25, but that's not the point). Since that broadcast, I have received many emails and letters from people wanting to know how to do this. Not only do these people know little about investing (let alone mutual funds), they make it clear that the reason they want to open an account with $100 is because $100 is all they have. Now, I talk less about account minimums and more about the importance of cash reserves and your need to eliminate credit card debt.

There's no doubt about it: The first thing you need to do is set aside sufficient cash reserves.

If you have no debt (other than a mortgage, which is really an asset class, not a debt) and have ample cash reserves, you are ready to allocate your remaining assets into a diversified investment portfolio. So, let's do so.

## SECOND, YOUR PORTFOLIO MUST BE HIGHLY DIVERSIFIED

Don't buy individual securities. Instead, use mutual funds and variable annuities.

That's what we do in our financial planning and investment management practice, which surprises some people. After all, my firm is the fifth largest independent financial planning firm in the nation, according to Bloomberg, and handles $1.7 billion in client assets. Thus, many people assume we trade stocks for a living.

But we don't. Instead, we use professionally managed accounts—mutual funds and annuities.

### Why You Should Use Mutual Funds

There are two reasons you should favor mutual funds over stocks. First, owning individual stocks is riskier than owning a stock mutual fund. That's because each mutual fund owns dozens, sometimes hundreds, of stocks.

A simple example demonstrates this. In the third quarter of 1999—remember, the overall stock market was still rising at this point—one in four stocks lost 20% or more. Yet, during that same period, fewer than one in a thousand mutual funds had such losses.

If you examine the performance of individual stocks during the 1990s—the most profitable decade in Wall Street history (the Dow increased threefold)—you'll find that 22% of all stocks lost money. Yet, during this same decade, only 0.4% of stock mutual funds lost money.

Everyone agrees that stocks are riskier than stock funds, but many people tolerate the risk in their effort to earn higher returns. That's where the statistics are the most startling. From 1990 through 1999, individual stocks earned an average annual return of 9.5%, while the average stock fund earned 15%. Thus, in that decade at least, mutual funds were both lower in risk and higher in return.

The second reason to use mutual funds instead of individual stocks is simply that there's more to a portfolio than stocks. If you think you're diversified because you own both small company stocks and large company stocks, you're kidding yourself.

Yes, you should own stocks—small caps, large caps, growth, and value. But you should also own real estate, international stocks, natural resources, oil and gas, and commodities. And the most affordable, efficient, and effective way to own them all is through mutual funds and variable annuities.

### Also Favor Diversification

Let's assume you have $25,000 to invest for 25 years, and you place equal portions of your money into:

- lottery tickets,
- a mattress,
- a bank savings account,
- a U.S. Treasury bill, and
- a basket of stocks that earns 1.3% less per year than the market's average from 1926 through 1999.

How much money will you have after 25 years? Well,

- You spent $5,000 to buy lottery tickets, and that money is gone!
- The $5,000 you placed under your mattress is still there, and it's still $5,000.

- Your savings account, which paid only 2% interest, is now worth $8,203.
- The T-bill earned 5.35% per year, so it's now worth $18,401.
- And that basket of stocks, which grew at an annual rate of 12% (compared to the stock market's 75-year average of 13.3%) has grown to $85,000.

You have a total of $116,604.

In contrast, if you had placed the entire $25,000 into T-bills that annually earned 5.35%, you'd have just $92,003—or nearly $25,000 less.

This remarkable result occurs even though you threw away one-fifth of the portfolio on lottery tickets, earned no interest on a second fifth, earned bank savings rates on the third and the T-bill rate on the fourth—and invested into stocks only 20% of your total assets. Imagine the results you could get with a more carefully designed and managed portfolio!

This is the glory of diversification. Placing 12 eggs in 12 baskets helps you reduce the risk of making a wrong investment decision or making a decision at the wrong time. Rather than regarding investing as a horse race (where you'd better pick the right horse or face losing everything), like most investors see it, you should regard investing as a game of horseshoes (where being close is good enough to win). Don't ever put all your money on what you hope will be the winning horse. Instead, place small bets on *every* horse.

History shows the benefits of this approach. Consider the 20 years from 1972 to 1993. This period includes the worst recession since World War II (the 1970s) as well as the great bull market that followed it (the 1980s). Imagine four investors. Throughout the 20 years:

- Investor A owned a portfolio of stocks.
- Investor B owned a portfolio of bonds.

- Investor C owned equal amounts of stocks, bonds, and cash.
- Investor D owned equal amounts of stocks, bonds, cash, foreign stocks, and real estate.

Who made the most money? A and D earned nearly identical average annual returns—the best of the four.

But whose portfolio was the least volatile? D's won by a landslide. D's portfolio was less than half as volatile as A's. Thus, D's portfolio earned equal returns but experienced far less risk.

This is the point I want to make about proper portfolio management. When we build portfolios for our clients, we're not trying to reduce their return; we're trying to reduce their *risk*. Indeed, seeking effective *risk-adjusted returns* is a far more important goal than seeking *returns* alone—as anyone who chased tech stocks in the '90s can tell you.

As September 11 has demonstrated, sudden declines in the financial markets can occur at any time. They can occur without warning, without predictability, and with sudden force. In times like these, the last thing you should have to worry about is how your investments are performing, for there are much more important things to focus on.

That is why you should build and maintain a highly diversified portfolio.

## FINALLY, HOLD YOUR PORTFOLIO FOR THE <u>LONG TERM</u>

Do you think the stock market will be higher in a month than it is today?

That's a difficult question to answer.

Here's an easy one:

Do you think the stock market will be higher in a *decade* than it is today?

And that says it all.

To invest successfully, you must adopt the strategy of a farmer: Plant seeds today and give them time to grow. Pulling them out of the ground and replanting them will not help them grow faster or taller. Instead it will reduce their yield while costing you more work and more money.

The same is true with investments. It is folly to buy an investment today and sell it tomorrow. The transaction costs, tax liabilities, and time involved make it extremely difficult to produce profits by frequently manipulating the investments within a portfolio.

I'm certain you agree with me, because whenever I ask people in seminars, everyone always claims to be a long-term investor. Unfortunately, most people aren't.

## Can Long-Term Investors Own Short-Term Investments?

Most people don't understand what "long-term" really means. It does not mean you have been investing for many years or that you will be investing for many years.

It means, instead, that *you will hold onto each of your investments for many years, even decades.*

There's a big difference between the two. I have come across thousands of people who claim to be long-term investors but who own portfolios in which every asset is less than six months old.

I have also met people who claim to be "long-term" investors but who plan to spend the money they've invested within a few years (or less) to pay for college or buy a home or for other needs. Money you're going to spend within three years belongs in the same places that you store your cash reserves; the only money you should have in investments is money you do not plan to touch for 5 to 10 years or longer.

**If you have money in investments that you plan to spend within three years, move that money to your cash reserves today.**

If everyone is a long-term investor, how can it be that in the 12-month period ending August 31, 2000, according to Forrestor Research, 42% of all the money in mutual funds was moved?

Clearly, a lot of people think *being an investor* is the same as *owning investments*.

Long-term investors who make short-term investment decisions—which I think describes just about everybody—are the most susceptible to making *bad* investment decisions. They buy when they should be selling and they sell when they should be buying. They worry about how investments will do in the next month instead of the next decade.

A lot of this is the media's fault.

No, let me rephrase that: A lot of the problem lies in the way most people listen to the news.

## THE MEDIA AND YOU

The media's job is to tell us what's happening right now. Like you, I have been very impressed with the media's performance in this crisis. They have been professional, reliable, responsible, and at the same time very human and sensitive.

But much of their coverage has also been shortsighted. I don't mean this as a criticism; it's the proper and necessary duty of news reporters to focus on now. So when the stock market reopened the Monday after September 11, the news fixated on that day's stock trading. The next day, we saw the headlines:

"STOCKS PLUMMET!"

But did stocks really plummet? The Dow's 700-point decline was only 7%—less than one-third as much as stocks declined in the Crash of 1987. This, despite the fact that September 11 was a far worse day for America than October 19, 1987, was. So, did stocks really plummet? Or could the headline have read,

> "CONSIDERING THE CIRCUMSTANCES,
> STOCKS PERFORM FAIRLY WELL!"

Is this headline any less accurate than the first? I think not. Instead, it all has to do with one's perspective. And the news media's perspective is firmly rooted in *today*.

In fact, several news organizations tried to be helpful, by showing viewers how the stock market fared in previous times of crisis. Bless 'em, they were trying their best, but they are not trained in personal finance. So when they tried to put September 11 into historical perspective by comparing it to other crises in our nation's history, here's what they did:

First, they identified those other crises. Their lists included:

| | |
|---|---|
| December 7, 1941: | Pearl Harbor was attacked. |
| June 25, 1950: | North Korea invaded South Korea. |
| November 22, 1963: | John F. Kennedy was assassinated. |
| August 8, 1974: | Richard Nixon resigned. |
| January 28, 1986: | The space shuttle *Challenger* exploded. |
| January 16, 1991: | The Gulf War started. |

The media showed us that on the day after each of these awful events, *the stock market fell sharply*.

Gee, thanks, fellas. Like we couldn't have guessed that's what happened—as if we expected stock prices to *rise* the first trading day after September 11.

What was the media's point in showing this information? Were they trying to scare us even further than we were already scared?

No, I think the media were just trying to be helpful by placing September 11 into some sort of historical context. The problem is that they chose the wrong context! Instead of showing how the markets did the day after prior crises, how about showing us how the markets did *one year* after those events?

After all, if we're supposed to be long-term investors, shouldn't we be more concerned about the long-term performance of investments through past crises?

I haven't seen anyone in the media report those statistics. So I had my staff find them. And, we discovered, here's what happened one year after each national crisis:

- One year after Pearl Harbor was attacked, the stock market was down less than 1%.
- One year after North Korea invaded South Korea, the stock market was up 14%.
- One year after President John F. Kennedy was assassinated, the stock market was up 23%.
- One year after President Richard Nixon resigned, the stock market was up 7%.
- One year after the space shuttle *Challenger* exploded, the stock market was up 31%.
- One year after the Gulf War started, the stock market was up 32%.

Changes your perspective, doesn't it?

As much as we're glued to the news these days, *we've got to get a grip.* Although we're living day by day, we must remember that investments are supposed to be evaluated not day by day, but year by year and decade by decade.

## WHY YOU LET EMOTIONS GUIDE YOUR INVESTMENT DECISIONS

Emotionally—remember, this is a book about emotions—we are worried, scared, upset, and anxiously waiting to see what the future will bring. We don't know what's going to happen next. We're all holding our breath, waiting. We know something is going to happen, but we don't know what, when, where, or who. All this is very unsettling.

And if we apply today's feelings of uncertainty to our investments, if we continue to watch our investments bounce up and down as closely as we watch news of the war, we are going to make very bad financial decisions.

Let me give you an example from *Ordinary People, Extraordinary Wealth* to illustrate this. A class of MBA students was separated into two groups. The first was shown the performance of the stock market at six-week intervals over a 25-year period. The second group saw the same 25-year performance, but at five-year intervals.

The students were then asked to build a portfolio that they would hold for the next 40 years. The students in the first group invested into stocks an average of 40% of their assets, while the second group placed into stocks 66% of their assets.

As the experiment showed, the group who studied the stock market most closely had little confidence in it. After all, they saw 216 intervals, each representing just six weeks of market performance. As a result, they saw many declines throughout the 25 years.

But the group who had paid little attention—the ones who looked at the market only five times in 25 years, each interval displaying a profit—displayed much greater confidence in stocks.

This is why you must be careful when you read, watch, and listen to today's news. And this is why I often tell consumers who own mutual funds not to look at the performance in the newspaper, or check prices online, or read the statements they receive in the mail. The news might upset you, and that could cause you to make a bad decision, motivated not by careful analysis but merely emotional outburst.

I want to emphasize that your emotional outburst might lead you to buy as easily as sell. It's obvious, for example, that the airline and insurance industries are having financial problems as a result of this crisis. It has been reported that the airlines lost $270 million each day the airports were closed and that insurance claims will exceed $30 billion, making September 11 the worst economic disaster in our nation's history. (Previously, Hurricane Andrew held the record, with $16 billion in insured losses.)

## Should You Sell Your Airline and Insurance Stocks?

Some people have reacted by selling airline and insurance stocks. That's a ridiculous thing to do.

I've actually heard people say they believe all airlines are going to go out of business as a result of the economic losses they sustained after September 11.

Yeah, right.

Like, from now on, we all have to *drive* to and from California.

If the airlines' only problem is *money,* then they have no problem—because money is the one thing America has in abundance. Within days after the attack, in fact, President Bush asked Congress for $20 billion in emergency funding. Congress gave him $40 billion.

That's just the beginning of the economic rescue packages Congress and the president are going to provide. If we were unwilling to let a single car manufacturer go out of business (remember Chrysler in the 1970s?), there is no way we'll allow our entire airline industry to suffer that fate.

Worries over the insurance industry are equally unnecessary. Yes, the $30 billion in claims will be higher than any other disaster to date. But let's remember that insurance companies have combined assets of *three trillion dollars.* To these guys, $30 billion is petty cash! Insurance companies are immensely profitable organizations—that's why you hate them, remember?—so they will not have any difficulty paying these claims.

When the insurance companies write those checks, guess where the checks go? Right into the pocketbooks of American consumers, who will spend that money in the American economy, rebuilding their lives and their businesses. This is one reason why the economy is going to grow in the future—the insurance industry is joining the federal government in providing us with a huge infusion of cash.

In the immediate aftermath of the attacks, people also started to worry that insurance companies would refuse to pay claims by invoking a "war exclusion" clause that exists in most contracts. If we're at war, the rumors went, insurance claims are void. It's nonsense, and every chief executive of every major insurance company in America has publicly announced that the company will not attempt to dodge its responsibilities to policyholders; all have publicly disavowed any suggestion of hiding behind a war exclusion clause.

A second rumor had it that death benefits wouldn't be paid, because death certificates aren't issued until a victim's body is recovered. Ordinarily this is true, but these are not ordinary times. Already, New York Mayor Rudy Giuliani has begun arranging for the distribution of death certificates, and insurance companies have already stated that they will not withhold payment of claims that lack them.

These are difficult times, and America's insurance companies are doing their part to help America rebuild. We all love to hate insurance companies, but when we need them, we're grateful and thankful that they are there and that they operate the way they do. Just as America's economy will emerge stronger in the future, so will the financial condition of our nation's insurance companies.

## Should You Buy Airline and Insurance Stocks?

Although I am confident that the airline and insurance industries are going to survive and thrive in the future, don't assume that you should go buy airline and insurance stocks.

That's because there's a big difference between the airline industry and individual airlines. Consider this:

- In the early 1900s, there were about 200 automobile manufacturers. Would you have been able to predict which two of them would still be in business today?
- After World War II, it was clear that commercial aviation was here to stay. Pilots leaving the military flocked to the nation's biggest and best airlines: Eastern, TWA, and PanAm. Although the airline industry has grown immeasurably, none of those airlines are in business today.
- No one doubts the viability of the Internet. But does that mean that most of today's dotcoms will exist in the future?
- Who would have guessed that a kid building computers in his college dorm would become the world's largest manufacturer of PCs, and that the world's largest computer manufacturer would leave the PC market after totally failing in it? (I'm talking, of course, about Michael Dell and IBM.)

The list goes on and on. Yes, airplanes will fly, but that doesn't mean that today's airlines will fly them. Yes, the insurance industry will remain strong, but that doesn't mean some carriers won't fail. So don't attempt to cash in on the crisis by buying airline or insurance stocks—or defense stocks or any of the other industries that you think are about to become profitable.

Instead, remember that the key to your investment success is to build a *carefully designed, highly diversified long-term portfolio*. No part of that phrase says to speculate in stocks that *you* think are currently low priced and that *you* think are about to become higher priced. After all, whenever you brilliantly conclude to buy a stock, remember that you're buying it from another person who has brilliantly decided to sell it to you. One of you ain't so brilliant.

Investing is not about speculating. So if you weren't researching and buying individual stocks before, why would you want to start now?

Don't get cocky. Stick with professionally managed mutual funds. If you do, and if your portfolio is carefully designed, highly diversified and long-term, you'll do fine.

There is no question that our nation's economy will improve. As a result of this crisis, the economy will be stronger, because we'll have eliminated the excesses from it and be focused more on productivity and profitability.

The economy will ultimately win because it reflects the economic strength of the United States, a $10 trillion economy. Even more important, the economy reflects the strength of the American people, the strongest, the most highly educated, most highly skilled, best prepared, and most dedicated people in the history of the world.

This is not a time to be fearful or worried that we might be entering a recession. Instead, we should be excited about what is to come. Look at the business cycle since 1940, shown in the chart at right, and you'll see that rising stock markets dwarf falling markets.

So, if it's true that we're in a falling market, you should be excited about what's to come rather than concerned about what we're in at the moment. Because, as the chart shows, economically at least, this moment will surely pass.

This is why we need not fear what will happen to our economy or to our investments. As horrible a thought as it is—and forgive me for saying it so crudely and with such insensitivity—war boosts economies. It boosts industrial productivity, leading to full employment and massive spending.

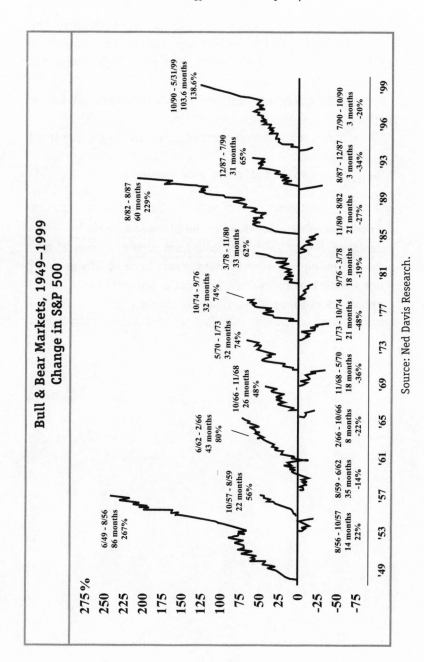

Bull & Bear Markets, 1949–1999
Change in S&P 500

Source: Ned Davis Research.

But war's economic gains come from the sacrifices of the members of our armed forces, the innocent victims, and all their families, and this cost is the very highest price. This is why you need to do only two things:

First, build a carefully designed, highly diversified long-term portfolio.

Then, ignore it and devote your energies and thoughts instead to your neighbors.

To learn how to do that, read the next chapter.

---

**I**f you haven't already done so, build today a <u>carefully</u> designed, highly diversified long-term portfolio—even if it means selling your current investments to do so. If you don't know how to build that portfolio, schedule an appointment today with a financial planner.

---

## CHAPTER 8

# No, You're Not Alone

B OY, DID *they* miscalculate.

If the cowards who struck all those innocent people thought they would intimidate Americans, they were wrong.

If they thought they would demoralize Americans, they were wrong.

If they thought they would fill Americans with fear, they were wrong.

If they thought they would create panic among Americans, they were wrong.

What they did was bring out the very best in Americans.

People everywhere have responded with love and generosity and acts of compassion to wonderful, heartwarming levels. Just as there are no words to adequately convey the horror of September 11, no words can come close to describing the unity, patriotism, community, and fellowship that all Americans have displayed so freely, so passionately, and so persistently in the days since.

As I explained in Chapter 1, you can do wonders for your neighbors, your community, and America's economy simply by going shopping, dining in a restaurant, seeing a movie, or taking a trip.

Within days after the attack, New York Mayor Rudy Giuliani, asked Americans to come to the city to support it economically in its hour of need. My wife, Jean, and I went to the Big Apple just 10 days later; I had a meeting to attend that had been scheduled months earlier, and the attack made us more determined than ever to go. The meeting wasn't until Monday evening, so we decided to go on Saturday and spend four days in the city. We took along two friends, Charlie and Carol, and lots of cash.

Like most people, I don't normally carry a lot of cash; credit cards are safer to use and more convenient (yes, there's a difference between using credit cards and accumulating credit card debt!). But I had emailed my editor at HarperCollins, Dave Conti, that I was coming to town. We booked a meeting and he closed his email by saying, "Bring cash."

I sensed that he wasn't joking.

Jean and I love New York City. We travel there several times a year, sometimes on business, often for pleasure. Our experience this time was unlike any other. We didn't see ground zero—we made a feeble attempt but were quickly shussed away by police—but that wasn't necessary to realize how deeply the attack on the World Trade Center has affected the entire city.

By New York standards, the city was empty. This is a relative statement, of course, because there are eight million people in New York. But the sidewalks, normally packed shoulder-to-shoulder, felt open and passive. Hailing a cab at any hour and on any obscure side street, typically a huge challenge, was a breeze. I didn't even have to wave my hand—just *seeing* me on the street was enough to bring a cab to my side.

Our hotel by Central Park was nearly empty. Much of the staff had been laid off, and those who remained told stories of what was happening at other hotels. Virtually all conferences and meetings had been canceled, leaving hotel rooms empty. While we were there, the nearby Plaza Hotel, a mecca for New Yorkers, actually closed the Oak Room. If you know New York at all, you've just gasped.

At one point, we traveled from Chinatown to Central Park via midtown, instead of using the FDR. That's an insane way to do it—that route normally takes 45 minutes to an hour because of New York's infamous traffic—but we did it in under 10 minutes. The only cars we saw were cabs, and many of them were empty.

Even Times Square was relatively devoid of people. At least four Broadway shows have closed, and many others played to half-filled seats. When a double-decker tour bus went by, the kind with open-air seating for sightseers, I counted less than a dozen people on board. They're usually packed.

The restaurants were equally bleak. Most were half-empty or worse. As in the hotels, the staffs were very happy to see us. In fact, the most memorable moment of our entire trip occurred at the outdoor restaurant atop the ice skating rink at Rockefeller Center.

Everyone in America knows this section of town, because Katie Couric and Matt Lauer host *The Today Show* from there—it's the place everyone stands waving signs and hollering to their friends back home. The area, needless to say, is always filled with people, and the restaurants in the immediate vicinity are always crowded.

But not on the morning we stopped by.

Because we had lunch plans already set, we just wanted coffee. There were only two other tables occupied, a most unusual sight for a beautiful morning in Manhattan.

We ordered and started chatting with the waiter, asking him how the restaurant had been doing since September 11.

Things were dreadful, he said. Normally, he earns $150 a day, but each day since the attack, he'd earned less than $50. He worried that things weren't going to change anytime soon.

He then disappeared to fill our order.

Now, $150 a day isn't much to live on in New York City. But $50 could quickly send a person into a financial abyss.

Later, when the waiter brought the check, Charlie and I decided to leave him a big tip. Although the bill was just $30 (okay, so we ordered a bit more than just coffee), we placed $150 in cash into the billfold.

The waiter came to collect, then left. A few minutes later, he returned and placed the billfold back down in front of me.

"Excuse me, sir," he said. "You've made a mistake."

"I did?" I replied.

"Yes," he said. "You put in too much." And he started to open the billfold to show me.

I waved him off. "That's okay," I said. "That's for you."

He looked at me quizzically. He clearly didn't get what I was saying.

"Keep it," I said reassuringly.

Slowly, his face showed clarity. He reached out his hand to me and said, "My name is Leo." And then he started to cry.

And we all started to cry, too.

New York is a wonderful place, surpassed only by New Yorkers. Jean and I will be returning soon. In the meantime, we're busy spending money in our local restaurants and shopping malls. I encourage you to do the same. And if you plan any travels, consider New York and Washington, D.C. Because the cowards targeted those cities, Americans in the surrounding communities have particularly suffered economically, and they need your help. But no matter where you go or what you buy, doing so will be a tremendous help to your neighbors, near and far.

---

**If you wish to donate money, President Bush asks that you visit www.libertyunites.org to find the names of groups who are providing direct help in New York, Pennsylvania, and Virginia.**

As announced on the cover, I am donating all profits earned from the sale of this book to aid relief efforts and other charities. *And other charities.*

Although the need for support is urgent for the victims of the attacks and their families, we must remember that others within our communities remain in plight. There are children who still have cancer, veterans who still are homeless, and persons in need all around us. Please don't forget the others who also need our help in these difficult times:

### *Arts, Culture, and Humanities*

- Humanities and historical societies
- Media
- Museums
- Performing arts

### *Education and Research*

- College and university
- Elementary and secondary
- Libraries
- Research institutes
- Vocational, technical, and adult

### *Environment and Animals*

- Animal protection, welfare, and services
- Beautification and horticulture
- Conservation and environmental education
- Health care facilities and programs
- Pollution
- Zoos and veterinary services

### *Health*

- Addiction and substance abuse
- Diseases and disease research

- Health care facilities and programs
- Medical disciplines and specialty research
- Mental health and crisis services

## Human Services

- Agriculture, food, and nutrition
- Crime and legal related
- Employment and occupations
- General human services
- Housing
- Public safety, disaster preparedness, and relief
- Recreation and sports
- Youth development

## International

- International development and relief services
- International human rights
- International peace and security
- Promotion of international understanding

## Public and Social Benefit

- Civil rights and liberties
- Community improvement
- Mutual/membership benefit organizations
- Philanthropy, volunteerism, and public benefit
- Voter education and registration

## Religious

- Buddhist
- Christian
- Hindu

- Islamic
- Jewish
- Religious media

If you want help in deciding which organizations to support, consult the following organizations:

### America's Charities

A coalition of the nation's best-known charitable organizations—groups providing direct services in thousands of local communities, across America and around the world.

AMERICA'S CHARITIES
14150 Newbrook Drive, Suite 110
Chantilly, VA 20151
1-800-458-9505
1-703-222-3861
Fax: 703-222-3867
www.charities.org

### Helping.org

An easy-to-use, one-stop online resource designed to help people find volunteer and giving opportunities in their own communities and beyond. With customizable services and comprehensive information, it's never been easier—or more secure—to donate your time, services, or financial support.

HELPING.ORG
c/o AOL Time Warner Foundation
22000 AOL Way
Dulles, VA 20166
www.helping.org

### GuideStar

A Web-searchable database of more than 850,000 nonprofit organizations produced by Philanthropic Research, Inc., a public charity founded in 1994.

GUIDESTAR
427 Scotland Street
Williamsburg, VA 23185
757-229-4631
www.guidestar.com

# WHAT TO DO NOW

Here's a summary of the action steps found throughout the book:

1. Hug your family, wave a flag, light a candle, go to church, say a prayer, give blood, make a donation, and *spend some of your money*.
2. Secure your debit and ATM cards.
3. Make sure you have cash reserves equal to a minimum of three months' spending, and preferably six months' or even a year's. Store this money where it is safe and readily accessible.
4. Buy a safe for precious and valuable items that you cannot replace, and keep a written inventory of these items elsewhere.
5. If you have equity in your house, take out a loan now and save or invest the proceeds.
6. Talk to your employer today about their plans for securing the company's viability in the event of disaster.
7. If you are a business owner or corporate executive, assemble your key staff and begin to implement disaster-recovery strategies today.
8. Compare today your current health insurance policy to the alternatives discussed in this book. If you don't think your policy is best, start shopping for a replacement immedi-

ately. If your employer provides your policy, talk with your human resources department about available options.

9. Avoid accident and dread disease Insurance; if you have this coverage, cancel it in favor of other, better policies (after confirming that you qualify).

10. Ask yourself: How much life insurance do you have?

11. Ask yourself: If you die, who would suffer financially?

12. If you are insurable, apply for life insurance today—before an accident, injury, or time makes you uninsurable.

13. Ask yourself: How long do you want to keep your life insurance policy? Your answer will help determine which type of policy is best for you.

14. If you have many older life insurance policies, see if you can exchange and consolidate them for newer ones. Doing so could save you money.

15. Even if you aren't absolutely sure which type of life insurance is best for you, apply for a policy *right now*. You can always change it later.

16. Buy disability income insurance today. Get help from a financial or insurance advisor when selecting and buying the policy.

17. If you are 50 or older, buy long-term care insurance. If your parents are over 50, make sure they have it. Seek a financial advisor's or insurance agent's help on buying the right policy.

18. Ignore government minimums for auto insurance policies and instead carry the maximums that your state permits.

19. Buy a homeowner's or renter's insurance policy today if you don't have one. Make sure your policy provides liability coverage of at least five times your annual household income or twice your family's net worth (whichever is greater). If you're a homeowner, make sure your home is insured for its replacement cost and that the policy reflects its current value.

20. If you live in an area susceptible to floods or earthquakes, make sure your home is insured against these risks. Get the coverage you need today.

21. Buy an umbrella liability insurance policy today.

22. Increase each insurance policy's deductible to save money.

23. Decide today "who gets what" in the event of your death. Then make an appointment with an estate attorney as soon as possible—preferably today. Tell the attorney about your plans or ask for his or her help in forming them. If you don't have a lawyer, ask your financial planner or tax preparer for a referral, seek names from friends or family, or contact your local bar association.

24. When you meet with your attorney, be sure to ask for a Living Will and a Durable Power of Attorney for Health Care. Sometimes these two documents are combined into one, called a Medical Directive.

25. When you meet with your attorney, be sure to ask for a Durable General Power of Attorney.

26. After granting someone your Power of Attorney, take a copy to your bank and financial advisor to confirm that they'll accept it.

27. Talk with your family today about your estate plan.

28. If you have money in investments that you plan to spend within three years, move that money to your cash reserves today.

29. If you haven't done so already, build a <u>carefully designed, highly diversified long-term portfolio</u> today—even if it means selling or repositioning your current investments. If you don't know how to create such a portfolio, schedule an appointment immediately with a financial planner.

30. You need to make a donation to help the victims of the attack and their families. Visit www.libertyunites.org to find the names of groups who are providing direct help in New York, Pennsylvania, and Virginia.

If you believe that any item on this list is important for you, complete it today. September 11 is a warning to us all that we might not get the chance tomorrow.

And here's the exciting part: although I've couched my advice in the context of preparing for war, the fact is that each of these steps can help you achieve substantial prosperity for yourself and your family. And that's really what we should be talking about, because even though our lives are changing in many fundamental ways—tighter airport security, for example—our lives are going to get better, not worse, from here on.

America is going through a difficult period, but we've gone through them before—and we'll go through them again. Our nation's greatness is not in our tall buildings or fancy cars or expensive clothes, but in the love and support we have for each other. Because no one shares our history, no one can challenge our future.

For in the United States of America, it is we, The People, who have formed a more perfect Union, established justice, insured domestic tranquility, provided for the common defense, and promoted the general welfare, *and we shall secure the blessings of liberty for ourselves and our posterity*.

Amen!

# INDEX

# ABOUT THE AUTHOR

ONE OF THE NATION's best-known and most successful financial advisors, Ric Edelman, CFS, RFC, CMFC, CRC, has earned three Awards of Excellence by Royal Alliance Associates and was named Ace Advisor of the Year by *Ticker* magazine, Financial Planner of the Year three times by World Invest Corporation, and one of the D.C. area's top financial experts by *Washingtonian* magazine.

*Inc.* magazine ranked his firm, Edelman Financial Services Inc., as the fastest-growing privately-held financial planning firm in the country three times, and according to Bloomberg, EFS is now the fifth-largest independent financial planning and investment management firm in the nation, handling $1.7 billion in client assets. The firm has won more than 50 professional, business, and community service awards, including "Service Business of the Year" by the Fairfax, Virginia, Chamber of Commerce, all leading to Ric's being named the 2001 Washington, D.C., Entrepreneur of the Year.

In addition to his achievements as a financial planner, Ric is one of the nation's most active educators in the field of personal finance. He is the bestselling author of the #1 *New York Times* bestseller *Ordinary People, Extraordinary Wealth,* as well as the bestsellers *The New Rules of Money* and *The Truth About Money,* named Book of the Year by *Small Press* magazine.

Ric also hosts two weekly radio and television shows (for which he won the Washington, D.C., A.I.R. Award for Best Talk Show Host), writes a syndicated news column, publishes a monthly newsletter, and created one of the most popular personal financial web sites at *www.ricedelman.com*. He also has produced a series of videotapes and audio cassettes on a variety of personal finance topics and writes an advice column for AARP's *Modern Maturity* magazine and other publications.

For nine years, Ric taught personal finance at Georgetown University, and he remains a state- and AICPA-approved instructor for continuing professional education. He is also a member of the NASD Board of Arbitrators.